NEW TESTAMENT
EVERYDAY BIBLE STUDIES

NEW TESTAMENT
EVERYDAY BIBLE STUDIES

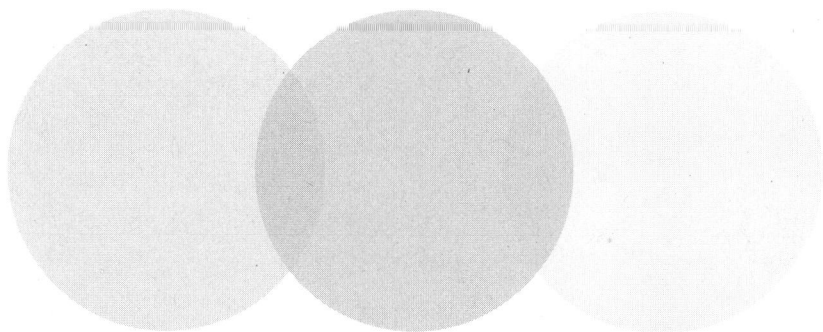

2 CORINTHIANS

LEADING IN THE MIDDLE
OF TENSION

SCOT MCKNIGHT

QUESTIONS WRITTEN BY
BECKY CASTLE MILLER

Harper*Christian*
Resources

New Testament Everyday Bible Study Series: 2 Corinthians
© 2024 by Scot McKnight

Published in Grand Rapids, Michigan, by HarperChristian Resources.
HarperChristian Resources is a registered trademark of HarperCollins
Christian Publishing, Inc.

Requests for information should be sent to customercare@harpercollins.com.

ISBN 978-0-310-12945-5 (softcover)
ISBN 978-0-310-12946-2 (ebook)

All Scripture quotations, unless otherwise noted, are taken from the Holy
Bible, New International Version®, NIV®. Copyright © 1973, 1978, 1984,
2011 by Biblica, Inc.® Used by permission. All rights reserved worldwide.

Scripture quotations marked CEB are taken from the Common English
Bible. Copyright © 2011 Common English Bible.

Any internet addresses (websites, blogs, etc.) and telephone numbers in
this study guide are offered as a resource. They are not intended in any way
to be or imply an endorsement by HarperChristian Resources, nor does
HarperChristian Resources vouch for the content of these sites and numbers
for the life of this study guide.

HarperChristian Resources titles may be purchased in bulk for church,
business, fundraising, or ministry use. For information, please e-mail
ResourceSpecialist@ChurchSource.com.

First Printing May 2024 / Printed in the United States of America
24 25 26 27 28 LBC 5 4 3 2 1

CONTENTS

For Northern MANT 2020

GENERAL INTRODUCTION

Christians make a claim for the Bible not made of any other book. Or, since the Bible is a library shelf of many authors, it's a claim we make of no other shelf of books. We claim that God worked in each of the authors as they were writing so that what was scratched on papyrus expressed what God wanted communicated to the people of God. Which makes the New Testament (NT) a book unlike any other book. Which is why Christians are reading the NT almost two thousand years later with great delight. These books have the power to instruct us and to rebuke us and to correct us and to train us to walk with God every day. We read these books because God speaks to us in them.

Developing a routine of reading the Bible with an open heart, a receptive mind, and a flexible will is the why of the *New Testament Everyday Bible Studies*. But not every day will be the same. Some days we pause and take it in and other days we stop and repent and lament and open ourselves to God's restoring graces. No one word suffices for what the Bible does to us. In fact, the Bible's view of the Bible can be found by reading Psalm 119, the longest chapter in the Bible with 176 verses! It is a meditation on eight terms for what the Bible is and what the Bible does to those who listen and read it. Its laws (*torah*) instruct us, its laws (*mishpat*) order us, its statutes direct us, its precepts inform us, its decrees guide us, its commands compel us, its words speak to us, and its promises comfort us, and it is no wonder that the author can sum all eight up as "his ways" (119:3). Each of those terms still speaks to what happens when we open our minds to the Word of God.

Every day with the Bible then is new because our timeless and timely God communes with us in our daily lives in our world and in our time. Just as God spoke to Jesus in Galilee and Paul in Ephesus and John on Patmos. These various contexts help us hear God in our context so the *New Testament Everyday Bible Studies* will often delve into contexts. Most of us now have a Bible on our devices. We may well have several translations available to us everywhere we go every day. To hear those words, we are summoned by God to open the Bible, to attune our hearts to God, and to listen to what God says. My prayer is that these daily study guides will help each of us become daily Bible readers attentive to the mind of God.

2 CORINTHIANS

INTRODUCTION:
READING THE BOOK OF
SECOND CORINTHIANS

Many remember vividly the experience of entering a room as a leader, a speaker, a worship artist, or a workshop organizer knowing that some in the room didn't like you, didn't want you to be up front, and didn't even want to be there themselves. Yet you have to be there. It's your job. Even what you are called to do. Paul was in that position often with the Corinthians. So, he wrote this letter both to win over the Corinthians to continue as one of his mission churches, to hope they would become more spiritually formed (12:19), and to persuade the Corinthians that some recently arrived popular preachers were toxic (11:5–6). In his attempts to persuade them, he trekked dangerously close to the steep cliff of defending himself too much.

Reading the Corinthian correspondence requires special sensitivities, so this Introduction is a bit longer than the others in the *Everyday Bible Study Series*. These two letters best fit the common description that goes like this: reading a letter of Paul is like sitting in a room with someone on the phone when all you can hear is one end of the conversation. And these two letters are not even always a conversation!

THE HEART OF PAUL

The Paul of the letters to the Corinthians is a vulnerable Paul with emotions and transparency. Read the following lines, mostly from 2 Corinthians, from Paul carefully. As you do, let your imagination seek an image of his face. What did it look like as he said these words, as his words matched his emotions, as he rehearsed his experiences and responses? As you read these verses, you may not be able to resist making the face you imagine he had. Go ahead, no one's looking.

> To this very hour we go hungry and thirsty, we are in rags, we are brutally treated, we are homeless. (1 Corinthians 4:11)

> . . . about the troubles we experienced in the province of Asia. We were under great pressure, far beyond our ability to endure, so that we despaired of life itself. Indeed, we felt we had received the sentence of death. But this happened that we might not rely on ourselves but on God, who raises the dead. (2 Corinthians 1:8–9)

> For I wrote you out of great distress and anguish of heart and with many tears, not to grieve you but to let you know the depth of my love for you. . . . Now when I went to Troas to preach the gospel of Christ and found that the Lord had opened a door for me, I still had no peace of mind, because I did not find my brother Titus there. So I said goodbye to them and went on to Macedonia. (2:4, 12–13)

We are hard pressed on every side, but not crushed; perplexed, but not in despair; persecuted, but not abandoned; struck down, but not destroyed. (4:8–9)

Make room for us in your hearts. (7:2)

Besides everything else, I face daily the pressure of my concern for all the churches. Who is weak, and I do not feel weak? Who is led into sin, and I do not inwardly burn? (11:28–29)

Paul was no stiff. He was an emotional man who cared deeply whether the Corinthians liked him or not. Homeless and without food at times; tested to the limit in confronting a possible martyrdom; full of "distress and anguish of heart and with many tears"; unable to preach the gospel because of anxiety over news about the Corinthians; pleading with them to love him; and full of pressure about all his churches.

Is this the Paul you picture when you think of Paul? Lots of people make disparaging remarks about this man. I suspect they have not read him carefully enough. My own attitude toward Paul mirrors my attitude toward the pastors of our family and churches, the leaders I have known. I respect them; I disagree with them; I get irritated. But I know they love us, they are doing their best, and no pastor and no apostle is perfect. A recent email I read from a pastor mentioned having "1,000 bosses." Paul knew that experience, too.

In these two letters, 1 and 2 Corinthians, you will meet the real Paul. His relationship with the Corinthians was not a happy one. At least not all the time. He's transparent about it, more than he even perhaps realized.

THE CONTEXT FOR PAUL'S LETTERS TO THE CORINTHIANS

The relationship between the founding pastor, Paul, and the believers in Corinth shifted from their barely tolerating him to their virulent criticism of Paul. What Paul wrote, with a pen burning letters onto papyri in our second letter to the Corinthians, gives us more than a glimpse of what the Corinthians, or at least some vocal critics, thought of Paul. In 2 Corinthians 10–13 Paul provides X/Twitter-like (very critical) clips of their criticisms of the apostle. (One of my students told me she gets on X/Twitter only to get angry.) To read Paul's criticisms of someone else's criticisms of himself is not always the easiest way to figure out the criticisms! We are not always reliable reporters when we describe what others think of us.

Take 2 Corinthians 10:1 as an example. Here Paul writes, "I, Paul, who am 'timid' when face to face with you, but 'bold' toward you when away!" The NIV puts timid and bold in quotations because the translators think Paul is quoting the words of the Corinthians. I agree. These words reveal that they accused Paul of being a milquetoast lightweight people-pleaser when present in Corinth in their house churches, but once he got back to Ephesus, he turned up the harsh tones of his opinions. A second example sounds like the Corinthians thought Paul's physical appearance did not stand up to their idea of a man with such rhetorical and social power: "You are judging by appearances" (10:7). Another indicates they thought he was unpolished and untrained as a public speaker: "his speaking amounts to nothing" (10:10; see 11:5). People-pleasing, unmanly, weak preacher. Not exactly the words you want to read in your Inbox when you wake up.

One of the more interesting criticisms concerned Paul's lack of boasting. This one indicates Paul lacked the kind of public bravado and self-confidence they expected of a traveling speaker. When he did go along with their custom of boasting, they poked him in the eye for it. "We are not going too far in our boasting . . . neither do we go beyond our limits by boasting of work done by others" (10:13–15). After all, it was Paul's gentile mission that snared the believers in Corinth, but Paul seems not to be taking proper responsibility for his accomplishments. They nail him for it. The flipside of Paul not taking sufficient credit for the wider sweep of his mission was that he was just too humble about it all: "Was it a sin for me to lower myself in order to elevate you by preaching the gospel free of charge?" (11:7). The people-pleasing, weak preacher lacked social confidence. When he did express confidence, his discomfort became an opportunity for criticism.

That raises the accusation they had with Paul about funding. He evidently did not take funds from them but "robbed," so they say, other churches when he ministered in Corinth (11:8; cf. 11:9–12). His principle was not to take funds when planting a church and refusing funds until the church was more self-supporting, and they thought this was a slam on their status. The Corinthians thought they were special, even high-status, a church full of "well knowns" and "who's whos." Paul was not impressed. His choice not to take their money degraded their status in their minds. They went full-on emotional on this one with a *You-don't-love-us*: "Because I do not love you?" (11:11). They also compared him to those Paul labels as "super-apostles" and he came up short (12:11). This one stung, so Paul pulled out his stinger and said, obliquely but the point is obvious, that he "persevered in demonstrating among you the marks of a true apostle, including signs, wonders and miracles" (12:12). *So, Corinthians, you think I'm inferior to these megastars, how about considering the miracles done among you.* That's oblique. What he means is *that I did some among you.*

5

Bonk! They even accused him of being a "crafty fellow" or "tricky" (12:16). It is not impossible they thought he did those miracles just mentioned by the powers of sorcerers! Ah, this sounds like accusing Jesus of exorcisms by the power of Satan (Matthew 12:24). Every corner he turned made for trouble.

So, the criticisms leveled against him by his own church parishioners included:

1. He had a weak, timid personality.
2. He was completely different, that is, he had a strong personality, when away.
3. He didn't have the right look.
4. His speaking and preaching skills were lacking.
5. He lacked self-confidence and had many self-hesitations.
6. He degraded their status by not receiving their donations.
7. He didn't love them.
8. He loved other churches more.
9. He wasn't on par with the more prominent Christian leaders.
10. He was tricky and slippery.

Plus, 1 Corinthians contains more of the same (e.g., 4:1–5; 9:1–23). Paul, as pastor and as apostle and as mentor, was anything but warmly received, respected, honored, and praised. He was talked about. He was gossiped about. They degraded him. As Paul Barnett says it, the Corinthians "didn't trust his *sincerity*. They questioned his *adequacy*. They doubted his *integrity*. They didn't acknowledge his *authority*" (Barnett, *Paul, A Pastor's Heart*, 55). But, as Barbara Brown Taylor observes with a wry reminder, "Everywhere he went he offended people, they said (which they, presumably, did not)" (Taylor, *Home By Another Way*, 171).

Everyone in the house churches of Corinth had an opinion about Paul, and it led to deep schisms. Divisions are common in churches. Pastors either put up with a lot or they move on, or in some cases they have good, nice people who mostly leave them alone. Any notion that the earliest churches were the golden age, or when it was done best, or full of fellowship and kissy-face harmony, must be junked today or sooner. Those churches were no different than ours: no better, no worse. Guy Nave says it right: "many Christians commonly romanticize the world of the New Testament and talk about the early church as though it represented a community of people who lived in complete harmony with one another. For many Christians, life was simple and uncomplicated back then" (Nave, *2 Corinthians*, 307). He's right about what people think, and the romanticizers get it very wrong.

THAT COMPLICATED
RELATIONSHIP WITH CORINTH

A woman named Chloe wrote to Paul with a bundle of questions and some information about how testy the relations were in the church, both between believers and house churches and between them and Paul (1 Corinthians 1:11–12). At the end of this letter, we learn that three men showed up and filled Paul in on what was happening in Corinth (16:17; Stephanas, Fortunatus, Achaicus). That was only the beginning of a series of trips back and forth, letters back and forth, and messengers from Paul to Corinth, who then returned with reports. In the middle of it all stands a courageous, persevering apostle who loves the Corinthians and longs for restoration with them.

Paul wrote a number of letters to Corinth. We have two letters in our New Testament, but many today have concluded that his (and our) second letter to the Corinthians combines two or more letters into one. Here's a brief outline of how it all took place, and the following is based on a lifelong specialist on Paul, Ralph Martin (Martin, *2 Corinthians*, 35–36).

1. Paul founded the church at Corinth AD 49–51 (Acts 18:1–17).
2. Paul departs for Ephesus (Acts 18:18–19).
3. **Letter A**, mentioned in 1 Corinthians 5:9. From Ephesus. We don't have this letter. (Is it perhaps behind 2 Corinthians 6:14–7:1?)
4. **Letter B**: Reports about divisions from Chloe's household (1 Corinthians 1:11).
5. Request from some in Corinth by letter for advice (1 Corinthians 7:1).
6. **Letter C**: 1 Corinthians, which responds to Letters A and B and more. Taken to Corinth by Timothy, who returns to Paul in Ephesus.
7. Timothy sent to Corinth for pastoral care (1 Corinthians 4:17; 16:10).
8. Crisis in Corinth; someone attacks Paul's leadership (2 Corinthians 2:5–11; 7:8–13). Timothy can't resolve the attack and returns to Ephesus.
9. Paul makes his painful visit to Corinth (2 Corinthians 2:1). Humiliated by their response to him, he returns to Ephesus.
10. **Letter D**: Paul writes the severe letter, which is at least reflected in 2 Corinthians 10–13. Titus delivered the letter. Titus requested to meet up with Paul in Troas.
11. Paul goes to Troas; Titus is not there; Paul proceeds to Macedonia (2 Corinthians 2:12–13).
12. Paul learns from Titus that the problem in Corinth is resolved (2 Corinthians 7:6–16).

13. **Letter E:** 2 Corinthians. From Macedonia. Titus delivers this letter.
14. More problems in Corinth (2 Corinthians 10:10; 11:27; 12:6–7). 2 Corinthians 10–13 may be the response to these problems.
15. Paul arrives in Corinth (Acts 20:2).

Paul's relationship with the Corinthians—trips back and forth, letters being sent, and the Corinthians not too happy with Paul—was complicated. Important details are not available, and specialists on these letters and the life of Paul do not agree. The fifteen points above, however, create enough impression to know readers of these two letters are in for a ride across bumpy waters.

FOR FURTHER READING

Paul Barnett, *Paul: A Pastor's Heart in Second Corinthians* (Sydney, Australia: Aquila, 2012).
Barbara Brown Taylor, *Home by Another Way* (Lanham, Maryland: Rowman and Littlefield, 1999).

DATING PAUL'S LIFE

Early Period: Who's in the Church? (48–57 AD)
Galatians (48)
What Are the Problems?:
1–2 Thessalonians (50)
1, 2 Corinthians (54, 56)
Romans (57)

Prison Ministry: What Is the Church? (53–55 AD?)
Philemon, Colossians, Philippians (c. 53, 54, 55
or 63?)
Ephesians (c. 55)

**Later Period: What Will the Church Be? (60–62 AD,
perhaps 64 AD)**
1–2 Timothy, Titus (c. early 60s)

WORKS CITED IN THE STUDY GUIDE

(Throughout the guide you will find the author's
name and title as noted in this book listing with
page numbers whenever I cite something from it):

Judith A. Diehl, *2 Corinthians* (Grand Rapids:
Zondervan Academic, 2020). [Diehl,
2 Corinthians]
Murray J. Harris, *The Second Epistle to the
Corinthians* (Grand Rapids: Wm. B. Eerdmans,
2005). [Harris, *2 Corinthians*]

Ralph P. Martin, *2 Corinthians* (2d ed.; Grand
  Rapids: Zondervan Academic, 2014). [Martin,
  2 Corinthians]
Scot McKnight, *Pastor Paul: Nurturing a Culture
  of Christoformity in the Church* (Grand Rapids:
  Brazos, 2019). [McKnight, *Pastor Paul*]
Scot McKnight, *The Second Testament: A New
  Translation,* (Downers Grove: IVP Academic,
  2023). [McKnight, *Second Testament*]
Guy Nave, "2 Corinthians," in *True to Our Native
  Land: An African American New Testament
  Commentary,* ed. B. Blount (Minneapolis:
  Fortress, 2007), 307–332. [Nave, *2 Corinthians*]
Philip Plyming, *Being Real: The Apostle Paul's
  Hardship Narratives, and the Stories We Tell Today*
  (London: SCM, 2023). [Plyming, *Being Real*]

LEARNING ON MISSION

2 Corinthians 2:12–3:6; 7:2–16

¹² Now when I went to Troas to preach the gospel of Christ and found that the Lord had opened a door for me, ¹³ I still had no peace of mind, because I did not find my brother Titus there. So I said goodbye to them and went on to Macedonia.

¹⁴ But thanks be to God, who always leads us as captives in Christ's triumphal procession and uses us to spread the aroma of the knowledge of him everywhere. ¹⁵ For we are to God the pleasing aroma of Christ among those who are being saved and those who are perishing. ¹⁶ To the one we are an aroma that brings death; to the other, an aroma that brings life. And who is equal to such a task? ¹⁷ Unlike so many, we do not peddle the word of God for profit. On the contrary, in Christ we speak before God with sincerity, as those sent from God.

¹ Are we beginning to commend ourselves again? Or do we need, like some people, letters of recommendation to you or from you? ² You yourselves are our letter, written on our hearts, known and read by everyone. ³ You show that you are a letter from Christ, the result of our ministry, written not with ink but with the Spirit of the living God, not on tablets of stone but on tablets of human hearts.

4 Such confidence we have through Christ before God. 5 Not that we are competent in ourselves to claim anything for ourselves, but our competence comes from God. 6 He has made us competent as ministers of a new covenant—not of the letter but of the Spirit; for the letter kills, but the Spirit gives life.

7:2 <u>Make room for us in your hearts</u>. We have wronged no one, we have corrupted no one, we have exploited no one. 3 I do not say this to condemn you; I have said before that <u>you have such a place in our hearts that we would live or die with you</u>. 4 <u>I have spoken to you with great frankness; I take great pride in you. I am greatly encouraged; in all our troubles my joy knows no bounds.</u>

5 For when we came into Macedonia, <u>we had no rest, but we were harassed at every turn—conflicts on the outside, fears within</u>. 6 But God, who comforts the downcast, comforted us by the coming of Titus, 7 and not only by his coming but also by the comfort you had given him. He told us about <u>your longing for me, your deep sorrow, your ardent concern for me, so that my joy was greater than ever</u>.

8 Even if I caused you sorrow by my letter, I do not regret it. Though I did regret it—I see that my letter hurt you, but only for a little while—9 yet now I am happy, not because you were made sorry, but because your sorrow led you to repentance. For you became sorrowful as God intended and so were not harmed in any way by us. 10 Godly sorrow brings repentance that leads to salvation and leaves no regret, but worldly sorrow brings death. 11 See what this godly sorrow has produced in you: what earnestness, what eagerness to clear yourselves, what indignation, what alarm, what longing, what concern, what readiness to see justice done. At every point you have proved yourselves to be innocent in this matter. 12 So even though I wrote to you, it was neither on account of the one who did the wrong nor on account of the injured party, but rather that before God you could see for yourselves how devoted to us you are. 13 By all this we are encouraged.

In addition to our own encouragement, <u>we were especially</u>
<u>delighted to see how happy Titus was, because his spirit has been</u>
<u>refreshed by all of you</u>. [14] I had boasted to him about you, and
<u>you have not embarrassed me</u>. But just as everything we said to
you was true, so our boasting about you to Titus has proved to be
true as well. [15] And <u>his affection for you is all the greater</u> when he
remembers that you were all obedient, receiving him with fear and
trembling. [16] <u>I am glad I can have complete confidence in you</u>.

Special Note to the Reader: We begin in an odd place for this
study guide. We begin in chapter two's account of Paul's experience. But that story of his isn't finished until chapter seven.
So, we include both some verses from chapter two and more
from chapter seven. Here's why: the whole of 2 Corinthians
1–7 assumes the crucial moment in the narrative at work in
today's reading. You will notice the word "comfort" in today's
reading, and that term gets turned up when we get to the first
few verses of this letter of Paul's. So, join us in beginning with
the experience of Paul.

Book learning and experiential learning complement one
another. But they are not the same. What one learns
from the experience deepens the book learning or drives one
to the book for a wider experience. But book learning will
not lead to the depth of learning that experience alone can
teach. Take psychology, something I have some experience
in because my wife, Kris, is a psychologist. She read books
and took courses and exams. Then she did a practicum.
Then she became a psychologist at a clinic. Her book learning was transformed once she had clients. I know this only
in part because I once read a major book by someone named
Theodore Millon on psychological disorders. I understood
some of what he described, but I had no capacity to recognize the subtleties of actual diagnoses and utterly no idea of
treatment for the person.

On mission, with book learning both behind him and alongside him until his John the Baptist-like end of life, Paul learned the sorrows and joys, the ups and downs of ministry. Whatever he learned from scripture and from rabbis was radically reshaped by the experiences with new churches. Today's reading takes us to the heart of the apostle Paul, the apostle, the pastor, the Christian, the down-to-earth real human. Paul begins a narrative about himself to open our passage (2:12–13), which he interrupts only to resume some five chapters later, at 7:5–16. We have combined the two units because they form the immediate, emotional, pastoral context for the first seven chapters of 2 Corinthians. With these passages in mind, one can understand these chapters; without them, one cannot. To read chapters three through six well requires knowing chapter two's conclusion in chapter seven. Make sense? I hope it does.

THE PLAN,
EVENTUALLY FULFILLED

Instead of traveling to Corinth yet again (see Introduction, p. 1–11), Paul wrote a letter, Letter D, also called the Severe Letter, and it is entirely possible bits of it survive in 2 Corinthians 10–13 (which may be the Severe Letter). In Letter D, Paul was harsh, and he knew it. His emotions were torn to shreds wondering how the Corinthians responded and what they were saying. Titus took Letter D to Corinth for Paul with instructions to meet up with Paul in Troas. Titus read it and answered questions on behalf of Paul, and no doubt Titus pastored some very upset people. Paul planned another trip to Corinth through Troas, but when he got to Troas, no Titus. This is where we meet up with Paul in today's passage. Once he arrived in Macedonia (northern Greece today), Titus arrived, and the whole world exploded into joy.

EMOTIONAL PAUL

The opening may sound profoundly unspiritual or unprofessional. Like having a pastor cancel his sermon Sunday morning because of a personal sorrow—with the audience overflowing and anticipating yet another good word from the Lord. Paul says he got to Troas "to preach the gospel of Christ" and he discovered "that the Lord had opened a door for me" (2:12). Instead of walking through that door into gospel mission work, Paul's sadness, depression—"No peace of mind"—sapped his strength to preach. (In today's passage from the NIV (pp. 12–14), I have underlined expressions of emotions.) His sorrow was over the absence of Titus. But behind that was the torture of not knowing how the Corinthians responded to his Severe Letter. Torn apart, he moved on to Macedonia.

What happened when he got there was so utterly wonderful, he interrupted his personal story for more than four chapters. We pick him up now at 7:5. First, he restates how he felt when he got to Macedonia. He was even more worked up: "we had no rest" and were "harassed at every turn—conflicts on the outside, fears within." Sleep didn't arrive at full rest. He felt a troubling pressure both externally and internally. All he wanted was a report from Titus about the Corinthians. *Were they angry? Were they sad? Were they ready to bolt or revolt? Or did they take his warnings to heart and respond as Paul hoped? Were they back in good relations again?* It is fair to conclude that Paul was traumatized by the way the Corinthians treated him. (More on this in chapters ten through thirteen.)

His appeal to them to become vulnerable to him reveals more emotions: They have a big place in his heart (7:3), but he spoke with "great frankness" (7:4). He was encouraged by their response, which expression reveals what he is about to tell them when he resumes his personal narrative (7:4). His joy is abounding (cf. 7:7, 13, 16).

But God . . . through Titus . . . "comforted us." The word *comfort* reverberates in this letter, and we are about to return to the beginning of this letter to watch this term come into full view. That term in chapter one requires knowing our passage in chapter seven because it is chapter seven that gives rise to the comforts of chapter one. Emotions explode when Titus talks not only about the comfort he gives Paul but he learns, too, that the Corinthians were comforting Titus (7:7). "Comfort" is the emotion concept Paul uses for the feelings he was experiencing and the feelings he discerns that Titus himself felt. What Titus divulged to Paul was about their "longing" for him, their "laments," and their "zeal" for him. Hearing this, Paul sits in a pool of joy (7:7; McKnight, *Second Testament*).

He's not done with his emotions. As we drop down to verse thirteen, he continues with not only encouragement but "he aboundingly rejoiced at Titus's joy because his spirit was rested by all of you" (McKnight, *Second Testament*). He's joyous because Titus is joyous because the Corinthians are joyous. A win-win-win situation. Two verses later, Paul observes Titus's "empathies" for them, and he finishes off with two more expressions welling up: "I am glad" and "complete confidence in you."

This is the real Paul. A Paul whose heart was so attached to this troubled group of believers in Corinth that he failed as an evangelist, could not do what God made possible to do, traveled with a torn heart, and then utterly exploded with joy when he heard good news from and about Titus and the Corinthians. How people responded to him mattered. His own harshness clearly was not vindictive but grief-born pastoral care. The stereotype of a stoic, that is a person "indifferent to pleasure or pain," does not fit the character of

Paul (*Merriam Webster*: https://www.merriam-webster.com
/dictionary/stoic).

LESSONS LEARNED

Paul did not simplify life by reducing suffering and hardships
to God's predetermined, inevitable plans humans are to grin
and bear. Instead, by seeking to be faithful to God and by
resiliently pastoring onward, Paul learned about God, about
himself, and about others. I see seven fruits that grew on
Paul's pastoral ministry tree because of his difficult experience with the Corinthians. We discuss each briefly, but these
can become wonderful moments for each of us to ponder
what we are learning from difficult experiences.

First, his experiences remind Paul that, as a follower of
the crucified Christ, he is a defeated enemy, a "captive" or, as
The Second Testament puts it, God is the "one always parading
us" through the streets of the empire. He has been captured
by Christ and the gospel, he has been put on mission, and
his mission means he's always being led around by the Spirit
of God (2:14).

Second, Paul switches metaphors from being a paraded
slave to a fragrant "aroma," a term found several times
(2:14–16). Actually, Paul uses two smelly terms, both
probably evoking sacrifices offered in pagan temples: "good
aroma" (2:15; *Second Testament*) and "fragrance" (2:14, 16).
These smells, as it were, were life for believers but death to
unbelievers (2:15–16). To one they smelled good; to others
they stank. Guy Nave rightly points us to the power of sac-
rifice without glorifying suffering or diminishing injustices.
He writes, "More than two hundred years of resistance contributed to the defeat of slavery in America. Decades of
resistance contributed to the defeat of Jim Crow and racial
segregation. Decades of resistance in South Africa led to the

defeat of apartheid. While it is easy to become disillusioned by the continued social and economic oppression of black people around the globe, the resurrection of Jesus Christ and the successful struggles of black people throughout the world attest to the fact that oppressive powers cannot prevail forever" (Nave, *2 Corinthians*, 313). Many, if not most, of those black leaders resisted out of Christian convictions, and took courage by pondering the resilience of the apostle Paul.

Third, Paul comprehends his unworthiness to the task, both because of his past rejection of Jesus and the church and because he knows his ministry and "competence" is all due to grace and the power of God (2:16; 3:5). He says this yet again in 3:5–6. One of my students, with whom I correspond often, signs off his letters with "All is Grace." Indeed.

Fourth, Paul's learned that he's not to be a huckster of ideas, a profiteer of religious goods, or a brand on a platform. Instead, all he does is held up to the vision of God and his sentence is therefore complicated by its God-directedness: "we speak before God" and we speak "as from transparency, as from God in front of God in Christos" (2:17; *Second Testament*). He's real, as we have already noted a few times. He's not pretending, he's not trying to be like his spiritual heroes, and he's not fulfilling a role. He's Paul, of Tarsus, convert to Jesus, called to the gentiles and learning day by day what an apostle is.

We turn now to Paul's fifth lesson learned from his mission experience. His only commendation is the embodied recommendation of the Corinthians living as followers of Jesus in Corinth (3:1–3). Paul puts on his platform, not himself, but the Corinthians. He says it this way: "You yourselves are our letter, written on our hearts, known and read by everyone. You show that you are a letter from Christ, the result of our ministry." I as a teacher, you in your ministry, need at times to be measured by the life of those in our care.

That measure humbles each of us because each of us knows we've done well with some but not at all with others. One of the most painful experiences in ministry is when people choose to leave our church or, for me, when someone drops out of class. We can choose to ignore them and let them walk away or we can do some exit interviews. Griping occurs, of course, and leaders have to develop thick enough skin to handle criticisms. But we can learn from exit interviews (and student evaluations) about our weaknesses. If we listen only to those who like us, which is a constant temptation, but do not listen to those who don't like us or who drop out of the class, we will not develop new wings and fresher ways. The embodiedness of the Corinthians plays off the term "letter": they are not a *written* letter of recommendation but a *living* one, one written "with the Spirit of the living God . . . on tablets of human hearts" (3:3). What kind of letter of recommendation do our students and those in our care write?

Paul knows it's all by God's grace (lesson three) but, and here's his sixth lesson, knowing it is all grace does not mean he doesn't have "confidence," that is "persuasion with God" on the basis of what Christ has done for us and through us (3:4). He can look God in the eyes and sense that he is doing what God has called him to do.

What Paul learned most he saved until chapter seven, which fittingly is our seventh lesson (7:8–15). He learned that the hard thing about pastoral care can be saying the hard thing with the right motive. He had been direct, firm, and even tough. But he was not vindictive, punitive, or retaliatory. Those with power can be tempted with each on a regular basis. The problem in ministering to people is problem people. Many of us wish they'd go away. Paul told them what he thought was going on. Some no doubt were angered by what he said, but in humility they seem to have embraced Paul's rebuke of "the one who did the wrong" with a pastoral eye on "the injured party" (7:12). That person probably led the divisions, or at least the opposition to Paul (see Introduction, pp. 1–11). Paul's goal was "godly sorrow" that led to "repentance" (7:9–10). On the tree of Corinth, the godly sorrow leading to repentance produced branches with an abundance of fruits: "what earnestness, what eagerness to clear yourselves, what indignation, what alarm, what longing, what concern, what readiness to see justice done" (7:11). They listened in humility and openness, they learned, they embraced, and the embrace of the truth of God was used by the Spirit of God to transform their culture. They learned to pivot from their previous divisive ways to embrace the way of the cross as embodied and taught by Paul and Titus (see McKnight, Barringer, *Pivot*).

Appeal

If Paul were teaching a class of future leaders in a church, he'd tell his story and what he learned in order to form young pastors in the work of ministry. He knew the Book of books but it was experiential learning that led book learning inside to the heart. Which is why in 7:2 Paul makes his biggest heart-felt appeal: "Make room for us in your hearts." Or, as in the *Second Testament*, "Make space for us." He knows there are some hard things about ministry. Judy Diehl discusses the necessity at times of confrontation, which when done well is "distressing, potentially divisive, and agonizing" (Diehl, *2 Corinthians*, 261). Her advice, gleaned from 2 Corinthians, includes being firm, affirming what is good in the people, being accurate and honest, knowing the facts, following up, being gentle while being firm, reflecting Christ always, and using discipline only when all else fails (262).

What can be missed in this "Make room for us in your hearts" is how it was shaped by Paul's attempts to persuade the Corinthians. Making room is more than an emotional tug of the heart. The heart is more than the center of one's feelings. The heart is as much mind as it is emotion. Paul's letter was an act of persuasion if it was anything. What can be missed, then, is the clarity and compelling nature of chapters one through seven. Three and a half centuries later one of the most electric speakers in the history of the church, whose sermons are still read today, John Chrysostom, was known because he "had the hearts and ears of the entire population [of Syrian Antioch] wide open for him." Notice the combination of "hearts" and "wide open." How did Chrysostom compel such a large audience? One of his biographers, J.N.D. Kelly, wrote that his persuasion was so powerful because of the "clarity of his diction (said by a contemporary 'stylist of grace,' one Isidore of Pelusion, as 'unequalled'), the simplicity and picturesqueness of his imagery, and, above all, the sureness with which he, as a speaker of rare charisma, was able instinctively to touch their hearts and consciences" (Kelly, *Golden Mouth*, 82). I shall break down that very long sentence into bits. Paul, like Chrysostom, could persuade the Corinthians if his aim was the heart, if his words were clear, if his imagery captured the imagination, and if he could touch the people where they lived. I suspect Paul, though not with the educated finesse of a Chrysostom or a first century orator, scored well on each point.

But Paul had learned that ministry is more than preaching and more than persuasion. Kelly observes above that Chrysostom had personal "charisma," which was not slick or tricky. Genuine ministry is personal, relational, and it all springs from love or it falls flat. Paul vulnerably discloses to them that they "have such a place" in his heart and so much so "that we would live or die with" them (7:3). The real Paul needed love and affection from those he loved.

Paul was a heart. Persuasive at that.

QUESTIONS FOR REFLECTION
AND APPLICATION

1. What does reading Paul's personal story up front like this help you understand about the context for 2 Corinthians?

2. What is your impression of this very emotional portrait of Paul?

3. Before reading this section, how much had you thought about Titus? How does this increase your understanding of Paul's ministry network?

4. If you were measured as a minister, in whatever context you serve by the lives of those in your care, what results would you see?

5. How could you let your heart lead you in ministry?

FOR FURTHER READING

J.N.D. Kelly, *Golden Mouth: The Story of John Chrysostom—Ascetic, Preacher, Bishop* (Grand Rapids: Wm. B. Eerdmans, 1995).

Scot McKnight, Laura Barringer, *Pivot: The Priorities, Practices, and Powers That Can Transform Your Church into a Tov Culture* (Carol Stream: Tyndale Elevate, 2023).

SHARED FAITH

2 Corinthians 1:1–11

¹ Paul, an apostle of Christ Jesus by the will of God, and Timothy our brother,

To the church of God in Corinth, together with all his holy people throughout Achaia: ² Grace and peace to you from God our Father and the Lord Jesus Christ.

³ Praise be to the God and Father of our Lord Jesus Christ, the Father of compassion and the God of all comfort, ⁴ who comforts us in all our troubles, so that we can comfort those in any trouble with the comfort we ourselves receive from God. ⁵ For just as we share abundantly in the sufferings of Christ, so also our comfort abounds through Christ. ⁶ If we are distressed, it is for your comfort and salvation; if we are comforted, it is for your comfort, which produces in you patient endurance of the same sufferings we suffer. ⁷ And our hope for you is firm, because we know that just as you share in our sufferings, so also you share in our comfort.

⁸ We do not want you to be uninformed, brothers and sisters, about the troubles we experienced in the province of Asia. We were under great pressure, far beyond our ability to endure, so that we despaired of life itself. ⁹ Indeed, we felt we had received the sentence of death. But this happened that we might not rely on ourselves but on God, who raises the dead. ¹⁰ He has delivered us from such a deadly peril, and he will deliver us again. On him we have set our hope that he will continue to deliver us, [11] as you help us by your prayers. Then many will give thanks on our behalf for the gracious favor granted us in answer to the prayers of many.

I have long admired Paul's Spirit-empowered willingness to pastor people who did not like him. The Corinthians were unquestionably shaped by a first century version of an upwardly mobile status-conscious society. Anyone who welcomed everyone into the assembly of Jesus, as Paul attempted to do, was sure to offend nearly everyone. Everyone, or nearly everyone, knew someone below them they'd rather keep down than welcome as an equal. So, the Corinthians had a history of giving Paul an earful and a hard time.

Once we have read 2 Corinthians 10–12 with an ear open to how the Corinthians treated him, we read passages like today's with a sense of surprise. What surprises me is that he did not begin this letter as he began Galatians where, following the formal niceties of greeting them, Paul launches into immediate rebuke (Galatians 1:6–10). In our letter, which we labeled Letter E in the Introduction, Paul opens with praise to God for the *experiences that united him with the Corinthians.* Shared experience was part of Paul's strategy for leading the Corinthians to unity in the middle of so much tension.

Paul, of course, opens with a standard letter introduction: authors (Paul, Timothy), identifiers (apostle, brother), and recipients. Paul *and* Timothy. Paul knows he and coworker Timothy are responsible for this letter. Paul, true to form in his life, did not seek to get all the glory. He shared his platform. "Effective ministry is always," Guy Nave observes with clarity, "a collaborative effort," and then he adds value with sensitivity: "and coworkers should be recognized and acknowledged" (Nave, *2 Corinthians*, 309). He sends this letter to the "church of God in Corinth" and then adds "together with all his holy people throughout Achaia" (2 Corinthians 1:1). Think of that. This very personal, pastoral letter will not only be read in Corinth's house churches but to all those in (modern day) central and southern Greece. We know of a church nearby in Cenchreae, home of Phoebe (Romans 16:1–2), but there may well have been others. He blesses all those churches with grace and peace (1:2).

SHARED EXPERIENCES

Paul uses two words to describe the Corinthian experiences: troubles and sufferings. The former leads to the latter. The Greek terms describe a variety of situations, from health issues to physical persecution to the final tribulation. But Paul provides the clues we need when he uses these terms for his own experiences in Ephesus (in Asia; 2 Corinthians 1:8). A big open window on what he experienced can be read in Acts 19:23–41, called the riot in Ephesus. Paul says he experienced "troubles" that involved "great pressure." I translate "great pressure" as "we were depressed–excessively, beyond ability" (McKnight, *Second Testament*). The emotional, psychological dimensions of his experience come to the fore when we use "depressed." So intense were these troubles that Paul says, "we despaired of life itself," felt he was issued "the sentence of death," and called it "a deadly peril" (2 Corinthians 1:8–10). Whatever Paul and others experienced, it was inescapable and unbearable. Some suggest what Paul experienced was the famous thorn in the flesh, which he experienced three times (12:7–8). Because these experiences edged so close to martyrdom, Paul describes them as "the sufferings of Christ" (1:5).

Paul's experiences and the Corinthians' experiences are so similar that Paul says they are the "same sufferings" they

"share," and the word "share" points to a common experience
(1:6–7). Paul capitalizes on that sameness to speak to the
Corinthians. The heat from those who worshiped Artemis
in Ephesus was similar to the heat some Corinthians were
experiencing. But we might add other experiences into
their troubles and sufferings, including some at the hand of
Paul's Severe Letter, which was painful to Paul and to them.
Referring to that Severe Letter, Paul describes it like this: "If
I caused you sorrow by my letter" that "hurt you" (7:8; Letter
D, p. pp. 12–14; look up 2:3–9; 7:8–12; 8:6). So, perhaps
their troubles and suffering involved Paul's pastoral rebuke.

And a word about social media, which constrains us to
tell good stories about ourselves, and how the smiley face
social media posts both fail to tell the reality and create
images that everyone is smiling. Paul does not write smiley
faces. He opens his heart to the Corinthians. Philip Plyming,
who has explored his own sufferings in light of Paul's, writes
about our human tendency these days to paint a rosy picture
of our own life:

> As I have read these passages in 1 and 2 Corinthians
> over the years, I have really appreciated Paul's hon-
> esty and openness. I say that because in some of the
> Christian circles I have moved in over the last 30 years,
> that hasn't been the case. I have often witnessed a pres-
> sure to emphasize the positive aspects of our Christian
> experience. 'I trust you're thriving!' starts the email,
> and it is quite hard to respond with anything other than
> the affirmative. At conferences, speakers are frequently
> unremittingly upbeat, and testimonies often end on a
> positive note. Christian organizations and institutions
> cultivate a reputation of growth and achievement;
> stories that point in a different direction rarely get a
> mention.

This pressure to emphasize the positive has been turbo-charged by a growth in social media, where so much attention is given to presenting an image that followers will "like." Along with so many Christians, we find ourselves telling a story in which we are doing well.

The image says we are thriving.

Yet my experience of the Christian life over the last 30 years has been much more mixed. I've witnessed some very positive things happen. I've seen people of all ages come to faith. I've seen people healed. I've seen individuals respond to God's call in their lives to do something new for the Lord. I've seen prayers answered and lives changed. I have known joy and hope and peace in my own heart.

But I've also seen much more challenging things take place. I've seen people walk away from faith. I've seen projects go badly wrong. I've seen partnerships fail amidst conflict and tension. I've attended and spoken at funerals in the most tragic of circumstances. I've seen people live with long-term illness and never get better.

This experience of brokenness has also been closer to home. I have reached points of real physical and emotional exhaustion. Anxiety, something that I have lived with since my teenage years, has at times been so bad that sleep has been very challenging.

I've also spent all my Christian life coming to terms with abuse that happened to me as a teenager. When I was about 13, I was groomed and then sexually abused by my parish priest. It was a secret, and I didn't tell anyone at the time. Like many survivors of child sexual abuse, I buried it deep within. Many years later I gave evidence in his trial, which resulted in a custodial sentence. But the experience of giving evidence was as traumatic as the original abuse, and I suspect the impact will be lifelong. (Plyming, *Being Real*, 3–4)

In light of Paul's own words about his own reality, we may need to redefine "thriving" from a happy, rosy life to a rugged life with ups and downs. A life in which God is present, not always felt as we want, but nonetheless always there. A life like Christ's. Like Paul's. A life in which "comfort" matters because of experiences of genuine pain and sorrow.

SHARED GOD

We enter a profoundly important theological distinction. If you mark your Bible, make some marks in 1:3–4 and 1:8–11 for each instance of God. As in "God of all comfort" or "He has delivered us." God is all over these verses. The Corinthians experienced suffering. Paul inserts God into their experience. Entering God into human suffering requires nuance and care. If one is not careful, one ends up blaming God for the experiences that lead to suffering. I don't believe it is morally justifiable to think God plots, directs, and causes the abuse of children and women. God did not toss the bomb on Hiroshima; God did not stir up Putin to attack Kiev. God does not send cancer cells into a body, nor does God block arteries that lead to heart attacks. I know many do think God does these things, but they make God a moral monster, someone who does what we as humans would never believe is right to do to another human. Humans violate the boundaries of other humans, but only a morally corrupted person thinks violating another is a moral good. Or that God violates.

So how do we nuance God in a discussion of suffering? We begin with God as unremittingly good, then we proceed to the human experience, then we remind ourselves God is good and just, and then we explain the suffering as some-thing *through which we learned to trust in God and how God preserves us and saves us and comforts us.* Explaining vio-lence against an innocent person as an act of God creates both reckless and abusive theology. God does not *cause* the troubles or the sufferings in today's passage. God *comforts* those who are troubled and who suffer. Because we learn something valuable from suffering does not mean God causes the suffering to teach us that. I realize this paragraph may well challenge what some believe, so I ask you to ponder these words and discuss them with others.

The God who comforts is the "God and Father of our Lord Jesus Christ" (1:3), and this God "raises the dead," "delivered us from such a deadly peril," and "will continue to deliver us" (1:9–10). Such a God does not *cause* troubles or sufferings. Such a God *comforts* those who are troubled and suffering.

SHARED COMFORT

I have circled the word "comfort" in my Bible. Circles appear throughout 1:3–7. The one use of "compassion" (1:3; "sympa-thies" in *Second Testament*) complements the abundance of the term "comfort." As Judy Diehl makes clear, comfort "is not just a kind thought; comfort is concrete support through an affliction" (Diehl, *2 Corinthians*, 80). The support offered corresponds with the trouble or suffering experienced. It is "consolatory strengthening in the face of adversity that affords spiritual nourishment" (Harris, *2 Corinthians*, 143).

When Christians learn about, listen to, and empathize and sympathize with those who suffer, they enter the work God is doing in someone's life. If God is the God of comfort, and if the God of comfort is with us when we suffer, then when we comfort others, we participate in the comforting work of God. Give it up here for psychologists who have learned the art of listening, asking questions, and creating an opportunity for a person to find insight into themselves, their emotions, and their experiences. Give it up for pastoral counselors who have been trained to connect to persons both spiritually and psychologically. Give it up for ordinary believers with eyes to see and ears to hear who use both to console others. Give it up for parents who love their children by listening, mentoring, and co-regulating. Every person who comforts another is doing the work of God for the suffering and troubled.

A final reflection: Paul's comfort of the Corinthians derives from his experience of comfort by God. He was the mediator of the God of comfort to the Corinthians who were in need of comfort. What Paul learned from his troubles and sufferings was dependence on God. Experiences matter, and experienced or lived theology forms into the purest form of theology on offer. Experienced, lived theology forms wisdom, and what Paul offers in today's reading is the wisdom of one who has learned God's comfort.

QUESTIONS FOR REFLECTION AND APPLICATION

1. What experiences might have made up Paul's sufferings?

2. How did the Corinthians possibly suffer?

3. What is the difference between God *causing* suffering and God *comforting* those who suffer?

4. How have you experienced God's comfort in your sufferings?

5. Have you ever had to pastor, care for, or minister to people who didn't like you? What could you learn from Paul about such a situation?

FIRST THINGS
FIRST

2 Corinthians 1:12–22

12 Now this is our boast: Our conscience testifies that we have conducted ourselves in the world, and especially in our relations with you, with integrity and godly sincerity. We have done so, relying not on worldly wisdom but on God's grace. 13 For we do not write you anything you cannot read or understand. And I hope that, 14 as you have understood us in part, you will come to understand fully that you can boast of us just as we will boast of you in the day of the Lord Jesus.

15 Because I was confident of this, I wanted to visit you first so that you might benefit twice. 16 I wanted to visit you on my way to Macedonia and to come back to you from Macedonia, and then to have you send me on my way to Judea. 17 Was I fickle when I intended to do this? Or do I make my plans in a worldly manner so that in the same breath I say both "Yes, yes" and "No, no"?

18 But as surely as God is faithful, our message to you is not "Yes" and "No." 19 For the Son of God, Jesus Christ, who was preached among you by us—by me and Silas and Timothy—was not "Yes" and "No," but in him it has always been "Yes." 20 For no matter how many promises God has made, they are "Yes" in

Christ. And so through him the "Amen" is spoken by us to the glory of God. [21] *Now it is God who makes both us and you stand firm in Christ. He anointed us,* [22] *set his seal of ownership on us, and put his Spirit in our hearts as a deposit, guaranteeing what is to come.*

Good leaders are good planners. But good planners adjust their plans. People looking for weaknesses, in even a good leader, will point out inconsistencies in plans or in the execution of a plan. Divisive people will pitch a tent on the leader's adjustments and pound long nails into the ground to fix their complaints. Today's reading details one complaint of some folks in Corinth and Paul's response. Since Paul's explanation in 1:12–16 assumes the complaint, which does not appear until 1:17, we begin with the complaint. But the overall strategy for Paul was both to defend himself and even more to show that his plans and their execution were shaped by keeping first things first. When in the middle of relational tensions and accusation, we easily forget to keep first things first.

Accusation

We can begin then with the problem presented by Paul's critics. The accusation, *Paul is fickle*, arose because he adjusted his plans (1:17). Did he have to adjust, or did he make light of some previously announced travel plan? I suggest we give the Corinthians at least our ears. From the New Testament we find three sets of plans in Paul's travel plans from Ephesus to Corinth.

In **Plan A**, which is clear in 1 Corinthians 16:5 (below), Paul plans to travel from Ephesus to Macedonia, then down to Corinth and off to Jerusalem for the feast and delivery of the collection for the poor.

Plan A

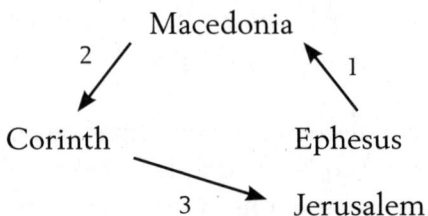

1 Corinthians 16:5

Plan B

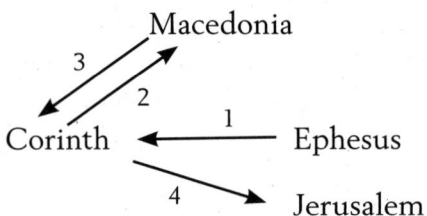

2 Corinthians 1:15

Plan C

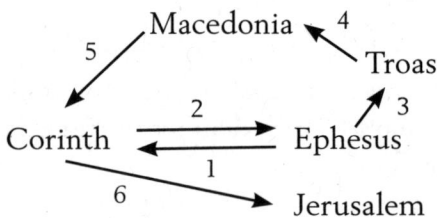

1 Corinthians 16:5   After I go through Macedonia, I will come to you—for I will be going through <u>Macedonia.</u>

Plan B changes Plan A and can be seen in 2 Corinthians 1:15. Instead of going north from Ephesus up to Macedonia (Plan A), Paul changed his mind (Plan B) and decided to come to Corinth first. He would then go north to Macedonia and back to Corinth before his departure to Jerusalem (thus, Plan B).

2 Corinthians 1:15   Because I was confident of this, I wanted to visit you [Corinthians] first so that you <u>might benefit twice.</u>

But instead of Plan A or Plan B as stated above, **Plan C** mixes and matches. Paul began with Plan B by first crossing the Aegean Sea to Corinth. But instead of going north to Macedonia, he returned to Ephesus (contrary to Plan B). Then from Ephesus he returned to Plan A, adding time in Troas. So, he accomplished both of his plans! Not so, thought some Corinthians.

In verse twenty-three Paul, no kidding, frames a nonexistent Plan D. Plan C routed a trip from Ephesus to Corinth, Corinth back to Ephesus, and then north. Plan D added yet another trip to Corinth from Ephesus after Plan C's return to Ephesus. In 1:23 he says he did not return to Corinth "in order to spare you"!

Fickle? Perhaps. *Flexible?* At least. But not fickle, according to Paul, for the one who surrendered plans to the Spirit. A flexible approach to plans appears in 1 Corinthians 16:5–7, with its "Perhaps" and "for a while" and "wherever I go" and "I hope to spend some time with you" and "if the Lord permits." Perhaps he was a bit fickle in his plans, so he offers an explanation. Plans are not as important to Paul as the Spirit's guidance.

EXPLANATION

We start with a ground level human reality. We have all been in situations in which one person's explanation seems entirely reasonable to them while our differing explanation is entirely reasonable to us. Welcome to Paul and the Corinthians in today's passage. The Corinthians think Paul is fickle; Paul thinks he's a straight arrow. Paul believes his conscience about relations in this world is clean. Even more so with the Corinthians. He examined himself and discovered "integrity and godly sincerity" (1:12; *Second Testament* has "with God's generosity and transparency"). In 1:15 he writes that he is persuaded of his own self-perception. He did not operate with "fleshy wisdom" (*Second Testament*; 1:12 and 1:17) but acted "on God's grace." His present letter confirms what he wrote before, which means he has not been fickle in communications (1:13). He believes they should both be co-boasting: they in him, and he in them (1:14). His conscience is clear enough that he felt good not only to visit once but twice (1:15–16). Paul thinks he's free of fickleness.

Though Paul's words are self-defensive, a charitable reading requires that we trust him when he says he examined his own conscience. We know some people appeal to their clean conscience when we think it ought not to be, but such self-examinations and their descriptions are subjective matters. Paul believed he was not fickle in plans or communications. More importantly, he has an entirely different way of framing his plans and back-and-forths with the Corinthians. His approach, which takes a reader a bit by surprise, is to appeal to first things first.

FIRST THINGS FIRST

In the middle of a committee or board and group discussion someone can utter or just mutter something like this: *Why are we even here? What is our mission? What matters most?* With the follow up: *We need to look at this specific decision in light of the gospel and our gospel mission.* Sometimes this changes everything. With the mission in view, previous discussions go away, new plans are formulated, and a clear direction is mapped.

The fickle accusation is that Paul's *yes* is not a *yes* but a *no*, and his *no* is not a *no* but a *yes* (see 1:17). In response, Paul shifts gears, speed, and lanes at the same time. Without even looking at the mirrors. He shifts from his necessary travel plan adaptations to the utter consistency of his "message" (1:18; "word" in *Second Testament*). Let's just say it: consistency of message does not mean plans are consistent. So be it, Paul's in a new lane. A lane where what happens to the gospel is more important than his plans. He adjusted his plans according to the gospel mission's needs.

He grounds his first things first gospel message in God remaining allegiant to his promise. Paul's message has singularly and faithfully been about "the Son of God, Jesus Christ" (1:19; cf. 1 Corinthians 15:3–5). Adapting their yes-no language, Paul says his message about Jesus is *consistently a yes*. God consistently utters the "Amen" and the "Yes" to Jesus. Paul's words are gorgeous and memorable: "For no matter how many promises God has made, they are 'Yes' in Christ. And so through him the 'Amen' is spoken by us to the glory of God" (1:20). God's "Yes" evokes Paul's "Amen." My friend, pastor Mike Glenn, wrote a wonderful small book about this memorable line called *The Gospel of Yes.*

Paul thus explains his adaptable plans on the basis of God's promises being fulfilled in Jesus. God's promises in

Jesus are the first thing, and plans are the second thing. The very One who solidifies Paul's plans and message is God, and this same God solidifies the Corinthians. How so? This God "christened us" (NIV: "anointed") and "sealed us" and "gave the Spirit-pledge in our hearts" (1:21–22; *Second Testament*).

The Corinthians may well have said to themselves, *We were right. Paul was fickle in his plans.* They also had to admit that Paul has been straighter than an arrow when it comes to the gospel of yes-in-Christ. The gospel message is more important than Paul's mission plans. First things first—a wise strategy, but it can get you into trouble, too. Just ask Paul.

QUESTIONS FOR REFLECTION AND APPLICATION

1. What was the accusation Paul's critics held against him?

2. How do you respond to someone who adjusts plans as Paul did? What is your verdict on Paul—fickle or faithful?

3. What is the first and most important thing to Paul?

4. How do you balance mission and planning in your ministry life?

5. How do you respond when people criticize your decisions?

FOR FURTHER READING

Mike Glenn, *The Gospel of Yes* (Colorado Springs: WaterBrook, 2012).

PAUL DID AND PAUL DIDN'T

2 Corinthians 1:23–2:11

²³ I call God as my witness—and I stake my life on it—that it was in order to spare you that I did not return to Corinth. ²⁴ Not that we lord it over your faith, but we work with you for your joy, because it is by faith you stand firm.

²:¹ So I made up my mind that I would not make another painful visit to you. ² For if I grieve you, who is left to make me glad but you whom I have grieved? ³ I wrote as I did, so that when I came I would not be distressed by those who should have made me rejoice. I had confidence in all of you, that you would all share my joy. ⁴ For I wrote you out of great distress and anguish of heart and with many tears, not to grieve you but to let you know the depth of my love for you.

⁵ If anyone has caused grief, he has not so much grieved me as he has grieved all of you to some extent—not to put it too severely. ⁶ The punishment inflicted on him by the majority is sufficient. ⁷ Now instead, you ought to forgive and comfort him, so that he will not be overwhelmed by excessive sorrow. ⁸ I urge you, therefore, to reaffirm your love for him. ⁹ Another reason I wrote you was to see if you would stand the test and be obedient in everything. ¹⁰ Anyone you forgive, I also forgive. And what I have forgiven—if there was anything to forgive—I have forgiven in the sight of Christ for your sake, [11] in order that Satan might not outwit us. For we are not unaware of his schemes.

P aul did a thing. He wrote a letter to Corinth. Paul also did not do a thing. He did not come to Corinth. What he did do caused pain; what he did not do could have caused even more pain. So, he chose to write a letter. That's 1:23 through 2:4. Today's reading reveals how Paul and the Corinthians were living with the implications of what Paul did, what Paul did not do, what the Corinthians did, and what they were to do next. Let's look at each.

WHAT PAUL DID

He wrote a severe, tearful, or painful letter. Severe in tone, painful to Paul, and painful to the Corinthians. Now that would be a piece of cake on a flat plate with a fork if it weren't Paul's letters to Corinth. Which letter is Paul talking about? Please keep your finger on this page and the Introduction (pp. 1–11) to sort out the details.

Letter A: 1 Corinthians 5:9–13 regarding
associations
Letter B: A Corinthian response letter (1 Corinthians
1:11; 5:1; 16:15–17)
Letter C: 1 Corinthians response to B (and A)
Letter D: Tearful or Severe or Painful Letter:
2 Corinthians 2:3–9; 7:8–12; 8:6
Letter E: 2 Corinthians, which could be stitching
together of letters, including Letter D!

We don't know, and I know I don't know. It's one of the first four letters mentioned above or a letter we no longer have. It's reasonable to see the Severe Letter in chapters 10–13, or at least something like the Severe Letter. What we do know is he wrote what he wrote to resolve the problems prior to arriving (2 Corinthians 2:3), and he wrote out of deep pain (2:4). He tacks on a bit later that he wrote that tear-drenched letter to test them, that is, to see if they could live as they ought to live as believers (2:9). Titus carried the Severe Letter (D) to Corinth.

What Paul Did Not Do

He did not come personally to Corinth. He wrote them, and the letter was a kind of personal arrival and presence of Paul. The one who read the letter to them represented Paul to the Corinthians. He did not go to Corinth so he would not have to make a second pain-causing visit. He spared them the confrontation (1:23). He quickly reminds them that he does not envision himself as one lording it over them but instead serves them as a coworker in the gospel (1:24).

What the Corinthians Did

They "punished" someone. The Greek term, however, has some social status implications, so I prefer the translation that they "dishonored" the person (2:6; *Second Testament*). This person had "caused grief" but Paul clarifies that the grief is not so much his but all of theirs (2:5). This makes it likely that the now-lost letter addressed someone who attacked Paul, which draws us into the kind of accusations we find in 2 Corinthians 10–13. So, the "majority" disciplined the attacker (2:6). Paul knew what they had done was both just and rectified the situation. So, he's pleased with what he did, what he did not do, and what the Corinthians did.

WHAT THE CORINTHIANS
WERE TO DO NEXT

Forgive the man and comfort him (2:7). Once the attacker-of-Paul had been

addressed or confronted,
admitted what he had done,
and confessed the sin,

the person was now in a place that could lead to forgiveness, comfort, and reconciliation. Reconciliation, as we are about to show, requires admission and confession. As Paul says it, "reaffirm your love for him" (2:8). Paul does not want them to grind him into "excessive sorrow" (2:7), but neither does he want them to offer cheap grace to a man who had caused such deep pain. What they forgive, Paul forgives. The Corinthians are trusted to mediate grace and forgiveness in Paul's place (2:10–11). Lingering vindictiveness gives place to "Satan" who wants to "outwit us" (2:11).

FORGIVENESS AND
RECONCILIATION

Forgiveness is a Christian disposition and action that can be very difficult to enact. Most today distinguish, very helpfully I believe, between forgiving someone and reconciling with someone. This helpful distinction is not expressed as such in the New Testament. The creative, grace-based theme of the New Testament is to be agents of forgiveness and reconciliation (Matthew 18:15–20; 2 Corinthians 5:16–21). However, repentance is required for reconciliation to occur in a healthy manner. To keep forgiveness and reconciliation

45

distinct, forgiveness has been understood as the act of releasing a person from the offense. With repentance needed, not to ignore sufficient healing in order to be present with the offender, reconciliation can become the next step. But neither forgiveness nor reconciliation should ever be demanded of the wounded, abused, and violated without (1) real repentance, (2) sufficient inner healing for the wounded person to safely confront the perpetrator, and (3) the requisites the perpetrator must follow for the reconciliation to occur. We recommend mediators to be present. A summary of this process looks like this:

Forgiveness occurs when:
a. an act violating a moral norm breaks trust, disturbs or destroys a relationship and, at times, produces moral outrage (resentment, anger, hatred, vindictiveness, righteous indignation),
b. is addressed at the level of morality, damage, and responsibility,
c. but, with full awareness of the gravity of the moral offense, an increased understanding of the personhood of the wrongdoer, and contrary to a retributive sense of justice, and based on one's own personal beliefs and personal health,
d. a victim chooses to release (suddenly or progressively) the moral outrage in various ways (emotionally, cognitively, behaviorally), depending on justice's and the victim's requirements (repentance, repair, restitution, retribution) and goals (psychological health, social justice, reconciliation) (adjusted from McKnight, "Slowing Down").

What seems so easy and simple can be enormously complex and complicated. Most of us are aware of the various elements of forgiveness and reconciliation. It helps at times to spell them out clearly. In the above you may observe a greater sensitivity to the victim who clarifies what is required for the relationship to be reconciled. This is sometimes called a survivor- or victim-centric approach. Such an approach begins with the victim. One must ask and listen to the victim; one must ask what the victim's health condition is; and one must ask the victim what she or he would like to see happen. Only then will a victim-centric approach create the grace that is needed. The sad reality in so many churches is that the offender or perpetrator is often given all the attention.

QUESTIONS FOR REFLECTION AND APPLICATION

1. Do you have a preferred theory about which letter is which, in sorting out the Corinthian correspondence?

2. Why should reconciliation include admission/confession?

3. What might be some of the benefits of the victim-centric approach to forgiveness and reconciliation outlined here?

4. Think of a time when you had to confront someone in a painful way, or someone confronted you. Did the relationship survive the confrontation? If so, how did it survive?

5. Have you ever tried to reconcile a difficult relationship? What happened?

FOR FURTHER READING

Works On Forgiveness

Lewis B. Smedes, *Forgive and Forget: Healing the Hurts We Don't Deserve* (2d ed.; New York: HarperOne, 2007).

Lewis B. Smedes, *The Art of Forgiving: When You Need to Forgive and Don't Know How* (New York: Ballantine, 1997).

Scot McKnight, "Slowing Down the Runaway Forgiveness Truck," https://www.booksand culture.com/articles/2004/julaug/19.36.html

Special Note to the Reader: Remember that you can find the Bible study passage for 2 Corinthians 2:12–3:6 on pp. 12–14.

THE PRIVILEGE
OF MINISTERING
TO OTHERS

2 Corinthians 3:7–4:18

7 Now if the ministry that brought death, which was engraved in letters on stone, came with glory, so that the Israelites could not look steadily at the face of Moses because of its glory, transitory though it was, 8 will not the ministry of the Spirit be even more glorious? 9 If the ministry that brought condemnation was glorious, how much more glorious is the ministry that brings righteousness! 10 For what was glorious has no glory now in comparison with the surpassing glory. 11 And if what was transitory came with glory, how much greater is the glory of that which lasts!

12 Therefore, since we have such a hope, we are very bold. 13 We are not like Moses, who would put a veil over his face to prevent the Israelites from seeing the end of what was passing away. 14 But their minds were made dull, for to this day the same veil remains when the old covenant is read. It has not been removed, because only in Christ is it taken away. 15 Even to this day when Moses is read, a veil covers their hearts. 16 But whenever anyone turns to the Lord, the veil is taken away. 17 Now the Lord is the Spirit, and where the Spirit of the Lord is, there is freedom. 18 And we all, who with unveiled faces contemplate the Lord's glory, are being transformed into his image with ever-increasing glory, which comes from the Lord, who is the Spirit.

⁴:¹ Therefore, since through God's mercy we have this ministry, we do not lose heart. ² Rather, we have renounced secret and shameful ways; we do not use deception, nor do we distort the word of God. On the contrary, by setting forth the truth plainly we commend ourselves to everyone's conscience in the sight of God. ³ And even if our gospel is veiled, it is veiled to those who are perishing. ⁴ The god of this age has blinded the minds of unbelievers, so that they cannot see the light of the gospel that displays the glory of Christ, who is the image of God. ⁵ For what we preach is not ourselves, but Jesus Christ as Lord, and ourselves as your servants for Jesus' sake. ⁶ For God, who said, "Let light shine out of darkness," made his light shine in our hearts to give us the light of the knowledge of God's glory displayed in the face of Christ.

⁷ But we have this treasure in jars of clay to show that this all-surpassing power is from God and not from us. ⁸ We are hard pressed on every side, but not crushed; perplexed, but not in despair; ⁹ persecuted, but not abandoned; struck down, but not destroyed. ¹⁰ We always carry around in our body the death of Jesus, so that the life of Jesus may also be revealed in our body. ¹¹ For we who are alive are always being given over to death for Jesus' sake, so that his life may also be revealed in our mortal body. ¹² So then, death is at work in us, but life is at work in you.

¹³ It is written: "I believed; therefore I have spoken." Since we have that same spirit of faith, we also believe and therefore speak, ¹⁴ because we know that the one who raised the Lord Jesus from the dead will also raise us with Jesus and present us with you to himself. ¹⁵ All this is for your benefit, so that the grace that is reaching more and more people may cause thanksgiving to overflow to the glory of God.

¹⁶ Therefore we do not lose heart. Though outwardly we are wasting away, yet inwardly we are being renewed day by day. ¹⁷ For

our light and momentary troubles are achieving for us an eternal glory that far outweighs them all. [18] So we fix our eyes not on what is seen, but on what is unseen, since what is seen is temporary, but what is unseen is eternal.

We all need to reserve occasional time slots in our schedules to ponder the privilege of spiritual gifts in the body of Christ. We need moments of remembrance. Frankly, routines and repetitions get tied into familiarity and frustrations. Ministry becomes a job, a task. We get measured by success. When those measures affirm us, we can easily become untethered from the inexpressible treasure and privilege of redemption itself and the calling to do what God calls us to do. I get up every day joyful in the privilege of more than four decades of my life studying, pondering, teaching, and preaching about Jesus Christ. Because of my age I know my career-end is on the horizon. Memories, and by no means are all of them good, sustain me at times, and they will sustain me after my teaching career is over.

Paul has a ministry-privilege moment in 2 Corinthians. The moment lasts from 2:14 through 7:1! This long section provides a look into the heart of someone privileged by grace to do gospel work. Paul realized, to use the words of Marilynne Robinson, he and his coworkers were "stewards of ultimate things" (Robinson, *Home*, 20).

Paul had a moment only because Titus had good news about the Corinthians that launched him into an extended discussion about the privilege of gospel ministry. Their response convinced the apostle Paul that God was at work, manifesting both his competency for the ministry as well as his confidence before God (3:4). Confirmation of God's work through him gave him a frankness or boldness about gospel work, both among unbelievers and believers. But Paul knew it was all grace. As Guy Nave reminds us, "No one is a minister of God because he or she is qualified or more talented than others. It is only because of God's mercy that one is afforded the opportunity of engaging in the ministry of revealing God's glory" (Nave, *2 Corinthians*, 314). In particular, the Spirit of God created a transforming new life in Paul and in others—Paul did not (3:6). This led Paul to reflect on the era of Moses as compared with the era of Christ, which then led him into a series of observations about the disposition of ministry itself. In today's reading, Paul does not walk a tidy line. He raises a topic, moves on, returns to the former topic, moves on, jumps ahead, and returns. We will do our best to sort out the themes.

ANCIENT VS. NEW COVENANT

His moment begins by reflecting on the gloriousness of the "new covenant" (3:6) when compared with the "ancient covenant" (3:14; *Second Testament*). Paul turns to bold contrasts between the two, but his contrasts derive from the gloriousness of the new covenant in Christ. He is not denigrating the law, Moses, or the ancient covenant. They were glorious (read Exodus 33–34). But, in comparison with Christ, they lack. It's like comparing a typewriter with a computer. In the typewriter days my IBM Selectric was awesome. When I got an Apple Mac (now a MacBook Pro), the IBM typewriter . . . well, all it wanted to be and more was found in the computer (except when the power dies). The typewriter was glorious until the more glorious computer arrived.

Old/Ancient Covenant	New Covenant

Moses	Christ/Spirit

Death (3:7)	Spirit (3:8)
Condemnation (3:9)	Righteousness (3:9)
Glorious/no glory (3:10)	Surpassing glory (3:10)
Transitory (3:11)	Lasts (3:11)
Moses, veil, dull (3:13–14)	Veil removed (3:14, 16)
Seen (4:18)	Unseen (4:18)
Temporary (4:18)	Eternal (4:18)

For God to assign to each of us the exercise of a Spirit-born gift is wonderful (see 1 Corinthians 12–14, refer here to my EBS *1 Corinthians*, pp. 169–175). Paul intensifies "wonderful" by comparing the ancient and the new covenant, or what can be called the First and the Second Covenants/Testaments. This provides for him a strong foundation on which to build a series of six dispositions for the use of spiritual gifts in the new covenant era.

The more Spirit and the more Christ, the less there will be of death, of judgmentalism's condemnation, of transitoriness, of a veil, of dullness, and what is visible and what is temporary. And the more Spirit and Christ, the more righteousness and surpassing glory and something that lasts as reflecting the unseen, invisible, eternal glory of God. And because of the surpassing glory of the Spirit's work among us, we are empowered to exercise the gifts God distributes among us.

We Can Exercise Gifts with a Hope-Propelled Boldness

Since I don't have them, I'm told it takes time to develop sea legs. That is, to stand or work on a boat without going dizzy and pitching meals overboard. Each of us needs time to develop competency and confidence in the exercise of a spiritual gift. I've watched students morph from eager-but-hesitant and called-but-unconfident into competent and confident dispensers of the gifts the Spirit bestowed on them.

At the heart of his exercising a Spirit-prompted gift is exactly what drove Paul into depression: he needed the Corinthians to respond affirmingly to his message, his ministry, and his Severe Letter. Without their affirmation, he could not preach the gospel in Troas even when he knew the Lord was at work. But once he hears good news from Titus *he suddenly has all kinds of confidence and boldness.* (Can anyone doubt Paul was an emotional apostle?) Boldness for Paul refers to frankness, the gift and capacity and skill to speak clearly with confidence (3:4, 12; 4:1–6; 7:4). This does not mean smarting off on social media or a blasting away at people. It means clear, firm, confident truth-telling. It means telling people about the gospel, that is, "the light of the gospel that displays the glory of Christ, who is the image of God" (4:4). He preaches "not ourselves, but Jesus Christ as Lord" (4:5). Which means not Caesar, not the local governor, not the procurators, not the high priests. God's message is the light of truth (4:6). Christian boldness is Christ-centered (4:5–6).

What his frankness overcomes is his former losing of heart, which can be translated with "negligent" (4:1, 16). The lack of conviction and confidence, often accompanied by depression, anxiety, and a general flatness in one's affect, can lead to neglecting one's gift, as Paul had just done in Troas. But Paul had been stirred by good news to reinvigorate his confidence and frank speaking about the gospel. We should not ignore Paul's decision to move away from Troas even when he knew the Lord had opened a door for him. He lost heart there but gained heart when Titus showed up with good news.

What kicked Paul's frankness into a higher gear was the energy from pondering the hope of the Christian. All of this is outlined in 3:7–11, which we detailed in the lists above, and 4:14. The resurrection of Christ entails the future resurrection of all those who are in Christ, including the ones who have lost heart and who are losing heart. Paul's hope is the resurrection, and that embodied new creation life to come stirred his gifts back into action. The surpassing glory and the eternal glory of the new covenant propelled Paul from despair into a hope-filled boldness. When a moment of realization pops into our hearts that tells us we are doing the Lord's work in the Lord's power on the basis of the Lord's future, we too can be propelled into boldness.

WE CAN EXERCISE GIFTS WITH FREEDOM

What a statement: "Now the Lord is the Spirit, and where the Spirit of the Lord is, there is freedom" (3:17). The Lord = the Spirit, which does not mean the Lord Jesus and the Spirit are identical persons. Father, Son, and Spirit are One and three at the same time. We need to tie 3:17 tightly to 3:16: the "Lord" who takes away the veil of 3:16 is the Spirit, and where this Lord Spirit is present *freedom abounds*. I agree with Murray Harris who says the freedom here is undefined and unlimited: freedom to speak frankly and boldly, freedom from the veil, freedom from ignorance, freedom from hardheartedness, freedom from the ancient covenant, freedom from the law's power, freedom to know and see God, freedom to be conformed into the image of Christ, and freedom of access to the presence of God without fear. And all these are discoverable, even if only partly glimpsed at times, in 2 Corinthians 3:12–18 (Harris, *2 Corinthians*, 312–313). Freedom doesn't mean doing what you want. The Spirit sets us free to do Spirit-shaped behaviors.

WE CAN EXERCISE GIFTS AS WE ARE TRANSFORMED

Maybe you grew up with an assembly line theory of salvation, which included not just regeneration but a specific order: justification came first and then sanctification and only at the End came glorification. The separation of justification from sanctification was not as healthy as the assembly line taught. But it did teach us to comprehend sanctification as more of a process of transformation. Whether you want to put this all into boxes on an assembly line or not, what Paul teaches is that we can exercise our gifts *while we are in the process of transformation*. We need to read 2 Corinthians 3:18 slowly and let it have its way: "And we all, who with unveiled faces contemplate the Lord's glory, are being transformed into his image with ever-increasing glory, which comes from the Lord, who is the Spirit."

Transformation, first, is made possible by the Lord, the Spirit. Second, we are transformed by gazing on the glory of the Lord by turning to the Lord. Third, the Lord transforms each of us, now or in glory, into the image of Christ. That is, transformation is Christlikeness. Finally, transformation carries a noticeable glory about it. Walter Brueggemann observes that for Paul transformation is the heart of the Christian life, when he writes, "Paul imagines that the Christian life consists in living close enough to God, attentive enough to God that the presence of God over time, through time, in time impacts us, changes us, heals us, makes us whole, makes us more like God's own self" (Brueggemann, *Collected Sermons*, 67). Transformation occurs only by being present to the God of glory in the face of Jesus Christ through the indwelling of the Spirit.

The glory of which Paul writes is not the lights of Broadway or the big ministry platform. Nor fame or the celebrity of being known for being known. It is the glory of God in the face of Christ being seen in us (3:18; 4:6). Getting better at our gifts is important, but that falls well below the mark if it does not also mean Christlikeness. What does Christlike look like? Read Matthew, Mark, Luke, and John. That's all we need, and that's more than enough.

Christlikeness takes a lifetime. No, it takes more than a lifetime because none of us will be "glory-fied" into full Christlikeness until the final kingdom. And I suspect we will continue to grow eternally as we encounter the infinite glory of the eternal Son of God.

WE CAN EXERCISE GIFTS WITH TRANSPARENCY

Paul informed the Corinthians that his life was an open book. He had repudiated secretive methods, he chose not to practice tricky techniques, and he put no masks on God's word (4:2). He wanted to put the truth on the table with clarity and pleaded with this audiences to give him feedback (4:3). But his message was not about himself, and he developed no brand. His "brand," if there was one, was not himself or his platform but the Lord Jesus Christ (4:5). He wanted to be known as the guy who walked and talked Jesus. He wanted to be the one whom people knew, if they got into a conversation with him, that they were going to hear about and see Jesus. He served others so they could see and hear from Jesus.

Frederick Buechner, in his wonderful book about preaching and the pastor, gave a word for all of us:

> If preachers or lecturers are to say anything that really matters to anyone including themselves, they must say it not just to the public part of us that considers interesting thoughts about the Gospel and how to preach it, but to the private, inner part too, to the part of us all where our dreams come from, both our good dreams and our bad dreams, the inner part where thoughts mean less than images, elucidation less than evocation, where our concern is less with how the Gospel is to be preached than with what the Gospel is and what it is to us. (Buechner, *Telling the Truth*, 4)

We can ask a question of ourselves: when we exercise whatever gift God prompts into use through us, do others see the gospel about Christ or do they see us? That is all.

WE CAN EXERCISE GIFTS WITH HUMILITY

I translated one of my favorite Bible verses like this: "We have this treasure in terracotta vessels so the power's excess may be God's and not from us" (4:7; *Second Testament*). Paul knew by experience the power of God at work through him to form churches, to instruct others, to participate in fellowship with believers, to share ministry with his coworkers . . .

he knew all of this and more. *But what he also knew was that it was all grace, all the work of God.* He knew he was a clay pot, colored by what looks like Georgia red clay. Terracotta pots and bowls are imperfect and fragile. Clay pots were beyond common; they were everywhere. They were useful. They were not fancy. Without paint they are not pretty. Paul's ministry, however glorious (3:7–11, 18, etc), meant the terracotta-like sufferings of all sorts. His terms here are "troubled" and "perplexed" and "chased" and "tossed down" (4:8–9; *Second Testament*). Gardner Taylor, that inimitable great preacher in New York City, knew the sorrows of life in the face of the Man of Sorrows. He told his congregation one day these words:

> Our faith is not a hothouse faith, off somewhere in a never-never land of innocent contemplation. The church of Jesus Christ was not born in a quiet ivory tower of isolated, insulated, and protected reflection. It was born in bloodshed and brutality, amidst nails, spears, hammers, lies, curses, gambling, and dark betrayal. The church came to be not by serene meditation alone, but it was jostled and pushed by the mystery religions of Egypt and Asia Minor, the hard-nosed, relentless logic of Greek philosophy, the harsh legalism and enmity of those who would not see and would not believe, and the brutal cruelty of the most ruthless empire the world has ever known: Rome. (Taylor, *Quintessential Classics*, 185)

Paul's life was death so the life of the resurrected Jesus could be at work in him and in others (4:10–12). This sounds like 2:14–16 and also like Galatians 2:20 and Mark 8:34–9:1.

I have held back here but it's time to say something. Too much of ministry, mine included, is about being noticed, about glory and fame, about social platforms and branding. Too many comparisons, too much competition for numbers.

Not enough is about Jesus and the glory of God in the face of Jesus. So, let's think together what we can do personally by way of intentional practices at reducing ourselves, not as a gimmick or in a fraudulent manner, but only so people can see Jesus through us instead of us.

If you are aware of the church's lectionary you will know that each week includes a reading from the Old Testament, a psalm or some verses from a psalm, something from a letter of Paul or the book of Acts, and then we all stand when we read the Gospel. Each week, every week of the year, and on each church holiday, we hear about Jesus. The sermons are not always about the Gospel passage, but I love that we hear about Jesus each week. Often the public reading of the Gospel is all I have needed to sustain me for the day and the week.

QUESTIONS FOR REFLECTION AND APPLICATION

1. How does Paul explain the new covenant as more glorious than the old, without putting down the old?

2. What role does hope play in Christian confidence and boldness?

3. What spiritual gifts do you have the privilege of using for God's people?

4. What was your experience in gaining your "sea legs" in confidently using these gifts?

5. How can you center the glory of God in Jesus through the exercise of your gifts?

FOR FURTHER READING

Walter Brueggemann, *Collected Sermons of Walter Brueggemann* (Louisville: Westminster John Knox, 2011).

Frederick Buechner, *Telling the Truth: The Gospel as Tragedy, Comedy, and Fairy Tale* (San Francisco: Harper and Row, 1977).

Marilynne Robinson, *Home: A Novel* (New York: Farrar, Straus and Giroux, 2008).

Gardner Taylor, *The Words of Gardner Taylor 3: Quintessential Classics* (Valley Forge: Judson, 2000).

BODY NOW, BODY NEW

2 Corinthians 5:1–10

[1] For we know that if the earthly tent we live in is destroyed, we have a building from God, an eternal house in heaven, not built by human hands. [2] Meanwhile we groan, longing to be clothed instead with our heavenly dwelling, [3] because when we are clothed, we will not be found naked. [4] For while we are in this tent, we groan and are burdened, because we do not wish to be unclothed but to be clothed instead with our heavenly dwelling, so that what is mortal may be swallowed up by life. [5] Now the one who has fashioned us for this very purpose is God, who has given us the Spirit as a deposit, guaranteeing what is to come.

[6] Therefore we are always confident and know that as long as we are at home in the body we are away from the Lord. [7] For we live by faith, not by sight. [8] We are confident, I say, and would prefer to be away from the body and at home with the Lord. [9] So we make it our goal to please him, whether we are at home in the body or away from it. [10] For we must all appear before the judgment seat of Christ, so that each of us may receive what is due us for the things done while in the body, whether good or bad.

Our bodies matter now. Our bodies will matter forever. Our eternal bodies are not identical to our bodies now. They will be remade to be fit for the presence of God in the kingdom of God. Our body-now will become our body-new. The correlation of persons born and persons dying is 1:1. Those in the body-now and those in the body-new correlate with those who are in Christ, the one who will (in today's reading) judge us (5:10).

So, embrace your body, work on your body, feed your body, enjoy your body, admire your body as the body God gave you. As the body God gave you to steward and enjoy. It is in this body that you live before God, with others, and with yourself. Know, too, that this body-now will get diseases, will decay, and will die, but the promise of God looks like the resurrection body-new of Jesus that we read about at the end of the Gospels (e.g., Luke 24:1–53; John 20–21).

One of my friends, a Black man, says African Americans wear their social uniform, their skin color that has been used by the dominant whites of our society as a weapon against Blacks. God will someday rip the false white uniform of the white supremacists off and rectify skin color as immaterial to worth and a cause of celebration for all. A Black body matters because God designed that body.

Many today, especially women, have the male gaze imprinted in their heads that judges their bodies according to male standards. Every woman's body matters to God. Some men do not have the bodies others think they should have, but their bodies matter to God. I cannot wish those body-images away, but I can say your body matters. God made your body. God calls you to live in the body as a child of God. You are your body. In your body you are the you God made. God also promises that the imperfections of your body will be perfected. Yes, it is true that some have ruined the

health of their body, damaged their body, and they sometimes feel shame about it. But God, the God who raised Jesus
from the grave, knows of Body 2.0 which we call in today's
reflections the body-new. Someday your body-now will be
God's body-new, just like Jesus' body.

BODY NOW

The rival, which had captured most thinkers of Paul's day, to
the Christian view of the resurrection was (various forms of)
Platonism. Platonism saw the body-now life as a trapping of
the soul, and at death the soul would be released into freedom from this slavish body. The Christian view challenged
Platonism's dualism. Christians believed that the body
would be resurrected. Most Christians probably believe in a
soul, but most theologians today think this form of dualism
misses the crucial integration of body and spirit/soul in the
Christian faith. Most speak of a soulish body or an embodied
soul, but not a body and a soul. Paul refashions the dualisms
of his day with an overt claim that the body-now will be
transformed into the body-new. Same but different; same but
not identical. What unites the body-now with the body-new
is the word body.

The body-now gets a variety of terms, each of which deval-
ues the body-now *but only because of the surpassing greatness of
the body-new*. It is, first, called "the earthly tent" (5:1). The
NIV drops the word house, so I translate it "earthly tent-*house*"
(McKnight, *Second Testament*), which permits us to see conti-
nuity and contrast between the body-now and the body-new
when in the second half of verse one Paul mentions "an eternal
house in heaven." With "tent" Paul evokes the impermanent,
temporary status of body-now. Second, the body-now is "mortal," which evokes dying (5:4). Third, body-now means we are
"at home in the body" and "away from the Lord" (5:6).

BODY NEW

In contrast to the body-now, the body-new has other attributes. First, it is a "building from God," an "eternal house," and "not built by human hands" (5:1). Second, our body-new is fashioned for an eternal duration by our body-now being "over-clothed" (5:2, 3, 4; *Second Testament*). Being "naked" for Paul means a soul without a body. To speak of being "naked" like that is a slur against the dualists of Paul's day. Third, it is a "heavenly dwelling" (5:2; the NIV adds another "heavenly dwelling" in 5:4 because that is implied). Fourth, the body-new is marked by "life" that replaces a body-now's mortality (5:4). Fifth, body-new means "at home with the Lord" and "away from the body[-now]" (5:8). Body-now becomes body-new only by the resurrection of the body (see 1 Corinthians 15).

Paul stuns those who want to think this world is all there is when he writes about "the one who has fashioned us" (or "prepared us") for this very purpose (2 Corinthians 5:5). We were made by God in order to become bodies-new fit for the eternal kingdom of God. That body could not decay or die. It must be the present body suited up for an eternal banquet.

LIVING IN THE BODY NOW

So, how to live in the body-now, knowing we will be outfitted with a body-new? Because the Spirit of God indwells us "as a deposit, guaranteeing what is to come" (body-new), in the present body "we groan, longing to be clothed instead with our heavenly dwelling" (5:5 and 5:2). As groaners and longers, we have "confidence" (5:6, 8) to "live by faith, not by sight" (5:7). That is, we live in the body-now knowing it will be the body-new. As faith-livers, we "make it our goal to please" God (5:9). In the body-now life we groan and we long

65

for the eternal body-new, and groaning and longing means living by faith as we seek to please God. We aim to please God because we will be judged by God for how we conducted ourselves in the body-now (5:10).

Groaning, longing, living by faith, and aiming to please God shape our "being renewed day by day" (4:16). Living in the body-now in light of the body-new transforms us away from materialistic bodies fit only for an earthly decay and the Grim Reaper. And knowing of the body-new transforms us into people who become fit by God's Spirit to indwell the eternal kingdom. The eternal kingdom will be designed for people who want to dwell in the presence of God, revealed in Christ, with others with the same desire. We are made fit for that kind of life by the Spirit of God who is at work in us.

Groaning is not about getting out of this body or leaving this earth. Groaning is the Christian's awareness that she is now understanding all that God has designed for her cannot be realized in the body-now. Groaning then does not mean degrading our bodies but realizing that we are made for more than we can now know. And we want it. At the same time, groaning is hope and confidence and the power not to lose heart (4:1–16). This groaning is not simply about things being better. Hope is about God making things right. The final kingdom of God, with us in a body-new world, will rectify all wrongs by eliminating evil, sin, and systemic injustices.

But groaning now is no excuse for waiting to do something about injustices now until the body-new world. No, groaning expresses the dissatisfaction of God's people with God's world and how unjust, unpeaceful, and sinful it is. Groaning prompts activism. Groaning prompts affiliations, coalitions, and organizations that work to rectify life in the body-now world so it looks more like the body-new world.

QUESTIONS FOR REFLECTION
AND APPLICATION

1. How did Christianity challenge Platonistic ideas of the body?

2. What are some of the differences between the body-now and the body-new?

3. How can we look forward to our resurrection bodies without looking down on our current bodies?

4. What challenges do you have in loving and accepting your body-now?

5. What activism is your groaning pointing you toward? How can you make the body-now world more like the kingdom of God?

THE RECONCILER

2 Corinthians 5:11–6:2

[11] Since, then, we know what it is to fear the Lord, we try to persuade others. What we are is plain to God, and I hope it is also plain to your conscience. [12] We are not trying to commend ourselves to you again, but are giving you an opportunity to take pride in us, so that you can answer those who take pride in what is seen rather than in what is in the heart. [13] If we are "out of our mind," as some say, it is for God; if we are in our right mind, it is for you. [14] For Christ's love compels us, because we are convinced that one died for all, and therefore all died. [15] And he died for all, that those who live should no longer live for themselves but for him who died for them and was raised again.

[16] So from now on we regard no one from a worldly point of view. Though we once regarded Christ in this way, we do so no longer. [17] Therefore, if anyone is in Christ, the new creation has come: The old has gone, the new is here! [18] All this is from God, who reconciled us to himself through Christ and gave us the ministry of reconciliation: [19] that God was reconciling the world to himself in Christ, not counting people's sins against them. And he has committed to us the message of reconciliation. [20] We are therefore Christ's ambassadors, as though God were making his appeal through us. We implore you on Christ's behalf: Be reconciled to God. [21] God

*made him who had no sin to be sin for us, so that in him we might
become the righteousness of God.*

*⁶:¹ As God's co-workers we urge you not to receive God's grace
in vain.*

² For he says,

> *"In the time of my favor I heard you,
> and in the day of salvation I helped you."*

*I tell you, now is the time of God's favor, now is the day of
salvation.*

In reading the passage above, you might be wondering what
chapter five has to do with the non-arrival of Titus in Troas
and the arrival of Titus in Macedonia. Paul interrupted, you
may recall, his story about himself at 2:14 and won't pick up
the story about himself again until 7:2. But chapter seven
is shaping chapter five. The very thought of Titus's arrival
bearing loads of love and good news (mentioned in 7:5–7)
suddenly shut down the story of Paul's experience and led
him to glory in what the Lord called him to do: the privilege
of being an apostle to the gentiles. Along the way, he has
mentioned the formation of his own confidence, hope, and a
hope-propelled boldness in gospel work. The foundation of
that hope is the resurrection of Jesus, and the manifestation
of that resurrection for believers is knowing their body-now
will become a body-new (5:1–10).

But, first, they must be assessed, evaluated, and judged
by Christ (5:10). Knowing the prospect of standing before
Christ—every Corinthian knew the massive size of the Bema
(judgment seat) in the center of Corinth—leads Paul to open
today's passage with these words: "Since, then, we know what
it is to fear the Lord, we try to persuade others." *Fear* before
God's righteous judgment and *persuasion* of gentiles form the

two crucial terms. *Fear* points at the awe, respect, and gravity of God's impartial, but ever generous, judgment. Paul worked at the art of *persuasion*, called rhetoric, so humans could be, now a third term, *reconciled* with God, with themselves, and with others—and so face the Lord's judgment in confidence and with joy. The God of judgment is the God who longs for reconciliation. So, fear leads to revitalized commitment to persuade others to believe in Jesus Christ so they can be reconciled.

Today's passage is all about the Reconciler, that is, God the reconciler whose agent of reconciliation is Christ and who gives to us, Christ's people, the mission of reconciliation. God as Reconciler should not, at least not very often, evoke God as mediating between warring parties or seeking compromise formed as a settlement. God acts to reconcile humans by sending the Lord Jesus Christ to resolve the problem and pave the path for the return of humans to God. And God's act of reconciliation begins with an individual, moves to groups, and because groups shape individuals, a reconciled group (the ideal church) becomes a culture that shapes individuals to become agents of reconciliation. So, everything in today's reading about you and me personally is about you and me together as well. It is both personal and group.

Today's passage leads us into the complex beauty of God the Reconciler.

GOD, THE RECONCILER

God makes not only the first move but the absolute most important move: "God was reconciling the world to himself in Christ" (5:19). I like to use the Greek word order here: (1) God, (2) was in Christ, (3) reconciling the world, (4) to himself. Reconciliation in the simplest of terms is a restored, flourishing relationship. Out of love for those whom God created and made, out of grace despite what humans had done, and all for renewed fellowship, God made the first move. His move was sending Christ, and in Christ, God made the first move. Nowhere else. The move God made in Christ was to reconcile the world, that is all of creation (Romans 8:18–30; Revelation 20–22). The work of God is not you and not me, but all of us. It's corporate, it's collective, it's social, it's cultural. To himself: God acts to bring humans back to himself. There is not a word here of what humans do. Humans don't reconcile with God. God reconciles humans to himself. Yes, humans only are reconciled because of grace-prompted responses of repentance and faith and reception and embrace. But so important for Paul is that God makes the first and most important move that he drops all hints of human contribution. God restores us to himself.

The actual reconciliation involves "not counting people's sins against them" (5:19). So, the premier act of God is to forgive humans—individually of personal sins and collectively of systemic sins. His language of "not counting" shifts from the interpersonal register of reconciliation into the register of commercial accounting: God doesn't calculate our sins against us *because our debt is erased by God's erasure.* "All this is from God" is how Paul opens verse eighteen and it serves here as the summary. God is the Reconciler.

CHRIST, THE AGENT OF RECONCILIATION

God reconciles. The agent of God's reconciling is Christ. God made him agent by the glorious interchange: "God made him who had no sin to be sin for us, so that in him we might become the righteousness of God" (5:21). Christ's "no sin" descends to us and our sin is transferred to destruction as we are lifted into Christ. This great interchange is what Jesus does for us in his life, his death, his burial, and his resurrection leading to his ascension to the Throne of God. Christ and we experience interchange.

Hang on for some tight language: He comes down to where we are so he can lift us out of What and Who we are to be like What and Who he is. We get What and Who he is, and he puts away Who and What we are (and were). He became what we are so we might become what he is. That's how Irenaeus, an early Christian father, explained the work of Christ for us when he wrote that Christ "became what we are, that He might bring us to be even what He is Himself" (Irenaeus, *Against Heresies*, Book 5 Preface).

CHRIST

HUMANS

That's the moment of moments with Christ as God's agent. We need to back up to discover the motive of the moment, that is, to verses fourteen and fifteen, where we read "For Christ's love compels us." There is some debate whether this is Christ's love for us or Paul's love for Christ. Paul's language is not clear, which is why another translation can reflect the magic of Paul's own language: "For Christos-love absorbs us" (McKnight, *Second Testament*). Which is it? Both. The Christos-love Paul has in mind immediately surfaces with this: he died and was raised for us (5:14–15). Not only that, he also died "for all" so that those who live the new creation life in Christ can live for the one who died so they may live! This, too, is part of the Great Interchange. It is not that we change places. The Great Interchange requires that Christ becomes sin so we become righteous. But—here is the

mystery—he becomes sin, or shoulders that sin, without losing his "no sin" or "righteous" nature. The greatest news of all
is that the one who shouldered our sin then dumped it into
the compost pile. Reconciliation doesn't begin until the truth
about ourselves—our human condition, our social condition,
our personal condition—is told.

This Christos-love, this Great Interchange in Christ,
switches in 5:17 to become "new creation." Suddenly dis-
covering our sin is removed and his righteousness is ours
simultaneously recreates us in the image of God to become
transformed into Christlikeness (3:18; 4:6). God the
Reconciler reconciles us by forgiving our sins, in Christ, and
so transforms us from sinners into transforming little Christs.
Great Interchange, indeed!

WE, THE PEOPLE ON THE
MISSION OF RECONCILIATION

Knowing that—as Jesus taught (Matthew 16:27)—each person will be judged by what they have done, Paul's mission was
to persuade people of the gospel. Let's pause to think about
this term persuasion. Persuasion has always been seduced
by manipulation. Persuasion shaped by coercion rather than
the freedom of the one being persuaded manipulates. Good
speakers with a good argument and a robust passion about
their message are the ones most in need of guarding themselves from manipulation.

Paul's persuasion included a witness to his own experience
of conversion to Jesus as Messiah, an explanation of scriptures
about the Messiah, some back-and-forth, an inquiry of people
and what they thought of Jesus, and he invited them to come
clean about their decision about Jesus. Paul was insistent that
he did not use devious rhetorical methods or manipulate his
hearers (1 Corinthians 3:19; 2 Corinthians 4:2), and that he

trusted God's Spirit to do the convincing (1 Corinthians 4:5). He wanted to live a life that was "apparent to God" and just as "apparent" to the Corinthians (2 Corinthians 5:11; *Second Testament*). But, in drawing attention to his own witness, he did not want to "commend" himself. Rather, he wanted the Corinthians to be persuaded in their own minds of the genuineness of his ministry (5:12–13). He wanted them to hear yet again that his motive was "Christos-love" (5:14). Frederick Buechner gathers these thoughts into memorable prose about the pastor's/preacher's task: "Drawing on nothing fancier than the poetry of his own life, let him [or her] use words and images that help make the surface of our lives transparent to the truth that lies deep within them, which is the word-less truth of who we are and who God is and the Gospel of our meeting" (Buechner, *Telling the Truth*, 24). That kind of persuasion, persuasive though it may be, has all the marks of genuine witness.

Paul's persuasion drew its strength from his new perspective on Christ and therefore on all of life. He has put in his rearview mirror everything in his past as "a worldly point of view," which was how he himself at that time looked at Jesus (5:16). It would be nice to get a detail out of Paul on this, but it appears he thought Jesus was a charlatan and corrupting the practice of the Torah (Acts 9:1–2; Galatians 1:13–14; Philippians 3:1–14). Following the encounter of Christ up close and personal, Paul's world view became Christocentric: he saw everyone in their relationship to Jesus Christ. This should not be reduced to *saved* or *unsaved* but to humans designed by God to become Christlike through the power of the Spirit.

Persuasion. World view. And now the mission of reconciliation. The work of God is to reconcile all humans to himself. As Paul wrote in today's reading back at 5:14: since Christ died for all, all have died. In Romans 5:18 Paul is a bit more explicit, so I quote him: "Consequently, just as one trespass resulted in condemnation for all people, so also one righteous act resulted in justification and life for all people." Paul was not a blatant universalist in the sense that all would finally be saved. But he did believe the act of God in Christ to reconcile the world was secured for all. The deciding factor, then, was whether the human made the uncoerced, free choice to embrace the plan of God in Christ.

With that plan in place, God "has committed to us the message of reconciliation," which is why he speaks of persuasion (5:19, 11) and of being "Christ's ambassadors" (5:20). This term sounds a bit more political than it is. The term is also used of mediators and negotiators. When we factor those senses into what Paul has in mind we get back to a more priestly-prophetic role for gospel agents. We are called to speak with God and for God as we mediate the message to others, and as we negotiate in the persuasion. So convinced is Paul of this mediating nature of gospel work that he says it's "as though God were making his appeal through us" (5:20). So, he now persuades the Corinthians in these words: "We implore you on Christ's behalf: Be reconciled to God" (5:20), imploring others to respond to Jesus Christ, which is not just a very serious act, but also sounds so much like preaching. I want to address a word to you about the value of preaching. The word I give to you comes from Dietrich Bonhoeffer in his candidacy sermon in a church in London in October of 1933:

> When a preacher opens the Bible and interprets the word of God, a mystery takes place, a miracle: the grace of God, who comes down from heaven into our midst and speaks to us, knocks on our door, asks questions, warns us, puts pressure on us, alarms us, threatens us, and makes us joyful again and free and sure. When the Holy Scriptures are brought to life in a church, the Holy Spirit comes down from the eternal throne, into

our hearts, while the busy world outside sees nothing and knows nothing about it—that God could actually be found here. (Bonhoeffer, *Collected Sermons*, 90)

"Every sermon," he said, and I would say, every encounter with the God of the gospel, "is basically an interpretation of that one sentence" found at the end of 2 Corinthians 5:20.

Frankly, that act of imploring them seems to assume the audience, the Corinthians, are not believers. The next verse makes clear he's talking about the saving work of Christ. How to explain? Is this evangelism for a moment? Has Paul switched lanes? I doubt it. I believe Paul's words about reconciliation are not evangelistic but pastoral. He is addressing a church-to-Paul relationship. Here are the indicators: first, he calls them "God's coworkers" in 6:1. That verse immediately follows his statements about reconciliation. The basis of their reconciliation is Christ's saving work. Second, in 6:11–13 he appeals to them once again to open their hearts to him. Third, the apostle Paul knows that salvation is more than the moment of getting saved but a comprehensive work of ongoing redemption and transformation. So, in 6:2 his words about "God's favor" and the "day of salvation" being "now"—these are words about his relationship to them, and their relationship to him. Salvation in this context is about reconciliation with God and with one another. God first, one another second.

It is fair to the text to see three reconcilers: God the Reconciler, Christ the Reconciler, and you and I on the mission of reconciling. Yet, our mission cannot be reduced to the evangelistic task of humans being restored in their relationship with God. Reconciliation that does not then expand into restored relationships with one another, with our enemies, and even into the public sector fails the reconciling work of God. God wants all to be reconciled with God, with oneself, and with others. The God, who is the Reconciler, wants an end to sexism, to patriarchalism, to racism, and to any form of social snobbery and status mongering. Paul doesn't go there but the God whom Paul preaches does, and we are called to go where God goes.

SENSITIVITIES ABOUT RECONCILIATION

Reconciliation matters. What matters as much is how we go about doing reconciliation. Intelligent Christians, working closely with psychologists, have learned to distinguish forgiveness from reconciliation. We know the first can lead to the second, and the second requires the first. But they are not the same. And different sensitivities are required for each. In a sermon at our church, our pastor outlined how we can lay the groundwork for forming a culture that reconciles. Her points were so helpful I include them here. She wrote her three important observations to me: "First, we lay the groundwork for reconciliation when we practice truth-telling, repentance, and forgiveness. Second, we lay the groundwork for reconciliation when we prioritize the restoration of those injured. And last, we lay the groundwork for reconciliation when we release our timelines for it" (Amanda Holm Rosengren, found at Substack below).

Amen.

QUESTIONS FOR REFLECTION AND APPLICATION

1. How does fear function in the life of a Christian, according to Paul's rhetoric?

2. What does it mean for Christ's people to have the ministry of reconciliation?

3. Why is the work of reconciliation a corporate effort?

4. What is the difference between persuasion and manipulation?

5. What aspects of the world immediately around you need reconciliation? How might God be calling you to bring reconciling work into that situation?

FOR FURTHER READING

Dietrich Bonhoeffer, *The Collected Sermons of Dietrich Bonhoeffer* (Minneapolis: Fortress, 2012).
Frederick Buechner, *Telling the Truth: The Gospel as Tragedy, Comedy, and Fairy Tale* (San Francisco: Harper and Row, 1977).
Amanda Holm Rosengren, scotmcknight.substack.com/p/readying-to-reconcile
Irenaeus, Against Heresies: https://www.newadvent.org/fathers/0103.htm

TO COMMEND OR NOT TO COMMEND

2 Corinthians 6:3–13

[3] *We put no stumbling block in anyone's path, so that our ministry will not be discredited. [4] Rather, as servants of God we commend ourselves in every way:*

in great endurance;
in troubles,
hardships
and distresses;
[5] in beatings,
imprisonments
and riots;
in hard work,
sleepless nights
and hunger;
[6] in purity,
understanding,
patience
and kindness;
in the Holy Spirit

and in sincere love;
7 in truthful speech
and in the power of God;
with weapons of righteousness in the right hand and in the left;
8 through glory and dishonor,
bad report and good report;
genuine, yet regarded as impostors;
9 known, yet regarded as unknown;
dying, and yet we live on;
beaten, and yet not killed;
10 sorrowful, yet always rejoicing;
poor, yet making many rich;
having nothing, and yet possessing everything.

11 We have spoken freely to you, Corinthians, and opened wide our hearts to you. 12 We are not withholding our affection from you, but you are withholding yours from us. 13 As a fair exchange—I speak as to my children—open wide your hearts also.

The desire of a leader, a speaker, a writer, a teacher, a parent—the list goes on—is to be received well. I don't write books like this with the expectation that either no one will read them or that everyone will dislike them. I want people to read what I write and gain from it. Of course, dialogue and disagreement are part of putting my foot forward. But the aim is readers whose lives are richer for the reading, for the engaging with this ragged old apostle Paul in his day. Which is not to say a leader's life goes into a tailspin when someone criticizes.

Still, Paul wears his feelings on his face in this letter. Judy Diehl connects the apostle to unrequited love when she writes that "unrequited love is the heartache theme not only of some sappy, romantic movies but also of many country songs. . . . Shakespeare used this theme magnificently in his dramas. In fact, much of human literature throughout the ages reveals a similar plot." Most don't connect Paul to unrequited love. Once you read today's passage you may make that connection. Judy and I both do. In our passage, "Paul became the caring pastor, focusing on the hope that his relationship with the Corinthians could be restored and that the church could be reconciled to him" (Diehl, *2 Corinthians*, 226).

TRANSPARENCY AND VULNERABILITY

Please notice Paul's words about his intentions and actions: "We put no stumbling block in anyone's path, so that our ministry will not be discredited" (6:3). He wants his audiences to encounter Jesus, not himself. But he's there mediating the gospel with a desire to create a culture of ministry that will not be able to "censure" his ministry (McKnight, *Second Testament*). Reputation matters until it matters more than transparency.

Skip down now to the end of today's passage. Paul must have stunned the Corinthians, ever concerned as they were with their status and protecting their (fragile) egos. He has spoken truthfully, transparently, and candidly—yes, he has. He has been vulnerable with them—too vulnerable, too open, some would say. He has not held his heart back (6:12–13). These are not the virtues of one embraced by *Romanitas*, the way of Rome, which was so systemic in the City of Corinth. He's too soft, too unmanly, too understated, too non-self-affirming. Instead of actively defending himself, he passively accepts opposition. Paul can take the negative and turn it into a positive (cf. 6:7b–10).

NOT COMMENDING AND COMMENDING

Despite Paul's desire and words that he wants things to be plain before God and plain before the Corinthians, and in spite of his desire not to commend himself (5:11–13), we get something at least a bit like that in today's reading. It's not easy to put "We are not trying to commend ourselves" in 5:12 with "as servants of God we commend ourselves in every way" in 6:4! Amiright? Just so we can see how detailed Paul is in his self-commendation (as a servant of God), I reformatted today's passage from the NIV into a list.

Here's what I think. Paul commends himself and his team "as servants of God" (6:4). He will not, as they do, assess himself as a status-measured success, not as someone famous, not as someone wealthy, not as someone with a book on the *New York Times* bestseller list (bought or not), not as someone with the biggest church in the Mediterranean, not as the best preacher with the most social media followers . . . you get the point. I do believe, even if it's a tad cringey, that Paul's non-commendations fit with his self-commendations *because of what he brags about.* That is, he brags about what the Corinthians think are disgusting reports about the apostle Paul. When you brag about your losses and oppositions you are not commending yourself, and you are cutting the legs off the statues on the street expressing *Romanitas.*

WILL YA JUST LOVE ME?!

I don't know with what tone you read the last line in today's reading, but here's how I read it: *Would you just please open up to me, accept me, embrace me? Will ya just love me?!* Does he not look a bit desperate? A bit too asky-feely? A bit lacking in self-identity? I can imagine a pastor with the elder board in a closed meeting. The tensions have been high. The pastor, with lips and chin quivering, and tears beginning to flow, looks around the room through filmy eyes and says, "Friends, I have loved you as best as I have been able. I love you now. Would you just accept me and love me in return?" Such is the tone needed to read 6:11–13. He wants mutually affirming affections in a "fair exchange" (6:13).

Paul may have been severe at times in his writing, but one thing is also true: the man had a big, soft heart for people and wanted to be loved in return and wanted the gospel's message to be embraced.

QUESTIONS FOR REFLECTION AND APPLICATION

1. What do you think of the idea that Paul had unrequited love for the Corinthians?

2. How does Paul subvert the Corinthians' ideas of Roman-style commendation?

3. In what ways does Paul put his reputation on the line in this passage?

4. If you were to make a non-commendation list about yourself, what would be on your list?

5. When have you exposed your heart to risk in asking someone to love you? How did it turn out?

A MISMATCH MADE
IN HEAVEN

2 Corinthians 6:14–7:1

[14] Do not be yoked together with unbelievers. For what do righteousness and wickedness have in common? Or what fellowship can light have with darkness? [15] What harmony is there between Christ and Belial? Or what does a believer have in common with an unbeliever? [16] What agreement is there between the temple of God and idols? For we are the temple of the living God. As God has said:

> *"I will live with them*
> *and walk among them,*
> *and I will be their God,*
> *and they will be my people."*

[17] Therefore,

> *"Come out from them*
> *and be separate, says the Lord.*
> *Touch no unclean thing,*
> *and I will receive you."*

[18] *And,*

> *"I will be a Father to you,*
> *and you will be my sons and daughters,*
> *says the Lord Almighty."*

[7:1] *Therefore, since we have these promises, dear friends, let us purify ourselves from everything that contaminates body and spirit, perfecting holiness out of reverence for God.*

Experts on 2 Corinthians all seem to agree—and that's rare—that today's passage does not fit. Or, at least, this passage switches lanes to change topics from what has been said so far. Maybe, maybe not. The relationship of the believers of Corinth with unbelievers has not been in the discussion so far. Separation from the contaminating influences of the flesh and the world were clearly at work in 1 Corinthians 5–6. But not so much in 2 Corinthians. Yet, today's reading echoes others in Paul's letters, like 1 Thessalonians 5:5 or Romans 13:12. It appears to me that the Corinthians' divisiveness and their resistance to Paul's message of reconciliation was shaped by their inability or unwillingness to turn away from the system of Rome. There is a whole lot of "them vs. us" in this passage. What happens when the "them" is *Romanitas* (the way of Rome)? Maybe that explains why Paul suddenly shifted lanes. The reconciliation problem running from house to house in Corinth was the *Romanitas* problem Paul had to confront. We believe Paul needs to clear the air before he resumes his exciting narrative about himself (7:2–4, and especially 7:5–16).

THEM VS. US

The "them vs. us" I mentioned above needs careful explanation. Paul's mind operates in systemic, not personal, categories.

Them: The system of this world, marked by the rejection of the truth of the gospel, forms into (1) unbelievers, mentioned twice, (2) wickedness, (3) darkness, (4) Belial, and (5) idols (6:14–16). These are terms Paul uses for those who have abandoned the gospel, or who have never embraced the gospel, for the ways of Rome and for the ways of his opponents.

Us: These vice marks of the world's system counter the virtuous marks of the pure message of God: (1) righteousness, (2) light, (3) believer, (4) Christ, and (5) the temple of God. These, too, are not personal and they don't describe every believer. This "Us" list forms the polar opposite of the "Them" list as Paul thinks in polar opposites.

So Choose

At the end of the Book of Joshua we hear an appeal and a public confession to make a decision for those who enter and live in the Land. Here's what we hear: "Now fear the LORD and serve him with all faithfulness. Throw away the gods your ancestors worshiped beyond the Euphrates River and in Egypt, and serve the LORD. But if serving the LORD seems undesirable to you, then choose for yourselves this day whom you will serve, whether the gods your ancestors served beyond the Euphrates, or the gods of the Amorites, in whose land you are living." And the confession is this: "But as for me and my household, we will serve the LORD" (Joshua 24:14–15).

Joshua's appeal formed into a paradigm for choosing to follow the ways of God when the people of God were tempted by the idolatries around them. This paradigm still speaks to us today in so many ways.

WHAT WE ARE

Centuries later the apostle Paul's appeal in today's reading resonates with Joshua's. Here's how Paul's works. First, he reminds them *what they are*. They are, because they are indwelt by the Spirit and engaged in a super-glorious ministry (2 Corinthians 3:7–18), the "temple of the living God" (6:16). The temple of Jerusalem has become contagious: its divine-presence purity and location spread to the people of God wherever they are. God both resides in them and walks around among them, and if this sounds like Genesis 3, it does. God makes covenant with them, for the words "I will be their God and they will be my people" are the covenant formula (Exodus 25:8; 29:45–46; Leviticus 26:12). God's covenant expands now to include the gentile believers in Jesus. We can expand the meaning of "temple" with another expression Paul uses: "new creation" (5:17).

It's Systemic, Not Personal

Second, he instructs them *to a systemic withdrawal* (6:17). But unless Paul is losing his consistent mind, he means here what he meant in his earlier letter to them. So, "I wrote to you in my letter not to associate with sexually immoral people— not at all meaning the people of this world who are immoral, or the greedy and swindlers, or idolaters. In that case, you would have to leave this world. But now I am writing to you that you must not associate with anyone who claims to be a brother or sister but is sexually immoral or greedy, an idolater or slanderer, a drunkard or swindler. Do not even eat with such people" (1 Corinthians 5:9–11). By "systemic withdrawal" I mean no longer adhering to the world's system, to *Romanitas*, the way of Rome. The Corinthians are not being asked to disengage from anyone completely. Engaging with persons one-on-one will not change; participating in the Roman, idolatrous way of life needs to change. No more celebration of the pagan gods, no more sacrifices, and no more living in the world's way.

A reminder about the meaning of holiness, which runs straight through the whole of today's passage: (1) God alone is holy, (2) God's presence makes something/someone holy, (3) when we give ourselves to God we are devoted to and we devote ourselves to the presence of God, which makes us holy, and (4) this three-step process of devotion requires withdrawal and separation from sin, systemic idolatry, and Satan. Holiness that emphasizes #4 without #s 1 and 2 and 3 is not biblical holiness. First God, then God's presence, then devotion to God, and only then separation from sin and the world.

PROMISES, PROMISES

Third, the *promises* of devotion to God, that is, to the way of holiness, are that God becomes our Father and that we become God's children (2 Corinthians 6:18). God's indwelling through the Spirit expresses God's adoption of us as children of God. We don't acquire these promises because we withdraw; we withdraw because the Spirit of holiness in us draws us out of Rome's system. The order in 7:1 expresses this perfectly: "Since we have these promises" we are called to "purify ourselves." This last verse in today's reading brings to expression the deep theology at work in the Christian's life of holiness. God is in us, God is transforming us, God transforms us away from *Romanitas*, and God transforms us to be fit for the presence of God. That's holiness.

QUESTIONS FOR REFLECTION AND APPLICATION

1. Who are the "them" and "us" in this section?

2. In what ways does Paul want the Corinthians to make themselves a set-apart people?

3. Read Leviticus 16:12, Isaiah 52:11 (or Ezekiel 20:34, 41), and 2 Samuel 7:8, 14 and ask why Paul chose those texts to quote to the Corinthians.

4. Have you ever been in a church that wanted you to withdraw from sin and worldliness but without first emphasizing God's holiness and our devotion to God? What might Paul have to say to that message?

5. How is the Spirit of holiness drawing you today?

Special Note to the Reader: Remember that we discussed 2 Corinthians 7:2–16 at "Learning on Mission," pp. 12–14.

PRINCIPLES OF THE CYCLE OF GRACE (1)

2 Corinthians 8:1–15

¹ And now, brothers and sisters, we want you to know about the grace that God has given the Macedonian churches. ² In the midst of a very severe trial, their overflowing joy and their extreme poverty welled up in rich generosity. ³ For I testify that they gave as much as they were able, and even beyond their ability. Entirely on their own, ⁴ they urgently pleaded with us for the privilege of sharing in this service to the Lord's people. ⁵ And they exceeded our expectations: They gave themselves first of all to the Lord, and then by the will of God also to us. ⁶ So we urged Titus, just as he had earlier made a beginning, to bring also to completion this act of grace on your part. ⁷ But since you excel in everything—in faith, in speech, in knowledge, in complete earnestness and in the love we have kindled in you—see that you also excel in this grace of giving.

⁸ I am not commanding you, but I want to test the sincerity of your love by comparing it with the earnestness of others. ⁹ For you know the grace of our Lord Jesus Christ, that though he was rich, yet for your sake he became poor, so that you through his poverty might become rich.

¹⁰ And here is my judgment about what is best for you in this matter. Last year you were the first not only to give but also to have

*the desire to do so. [11] Now finish the work, so that your eager will-
ingness to do it may be matched by your completion of it, according
to your means. [12] For if the willingness is there, the gift is acceptable
according to what one has, not according to what one does not have.*

*[13] Our desire is not that others might be relieved while you are
hard pressed, but that there might be equality. [14] At the present time
your plenty will supply what they need, so that in turn their plenty
will supply what you need. The goal is equality, [15] as it is written:
"The one who gathered much did not have too much, and the one
who gathered little did not have too little."*

Chapters one through seven were all about Paul's experience with the Corinthians. Chapters eight and nine
switch lanes abruptly into advocacy for generosity. I'm not
a fundraiser. If I were, I would want to build a Christian
approach to fundraising, first, by using these two chapters
and, second, by transforming fundraising into a Christian
understanding of generosity. Which does not mean reckless
giving. A Christian approach to generosity needs to consider
both the intake of funds and resources and the dispersal of
the same for the benefit of others. Wisdom leads us to think
of generosity as an ongoing life of giving that flows from a
lifetime of income, income that becomes a bank for a generous way of life. Paul is not against wealth or income. His
magnificent vision of generosity pushes against stinginess,
miserliness, hoarding, accumulation, indulgence, and half-
hearted giving. A sort of "gain all you can, save all you can,
give all you can" approach (based on John Wesley, "The Use
of Money," below).

For two chapters Paul urges the Corinthians to become
generous with their funds and resources to support the poor
saints, or "devoted ones" in Jerusalem (9:1; *Second Testament*).
We use many terms in the church: stewardship, giving, donations, offerings, tithes, etc. In another context, I wrote this:

"If Christ is Lord over all of life, if money and resources and possessions form one of the most important dimensions of life, and if pastors are called to nurture Christoformity in all ways, then the pastor is called to nurture economic Christoformity" (McKnight, *Pastor Paul*, 80). Paul, pasto rally, instructs in these two chapters about how to nurture generosity. I will focus on his principles and practices.

THE CYCLE OF GRACE

The Christian principle of generosity begins in one and only one spot: with God's generosity. The word "generosity" and the word "grace" overlap significantly in meaning. Even more so in Greek. Paul opens today's reading with this: "We want you to know about the grace that God has given" (8:1). This theme is deepened in 8:9 when Paul writes "For you know the grace of our Lord Jesus Christ, that though he was rich, yet for your sake he became poor, so that you through his poverty might become rich." God's grace is a gift that empowers, ennobles, and enriches the one lacking power, nobility, and wealth. The grace of God is an act of God toward humans who are stuck in sin and systemic sinfulness that both erases their sins and transforms them from sinners into generous saints.

Paul is at his theological best when talking about giving, because for him, donations are but a symptom and sign of God's grace given to humans. The expert on grace and gift in the world of Paul, John Barclay, a professor at Durham University, defines gift in these terms: "'Gift' denotes the sphere *of voluntary, personal relations, characterized by goodwill in the giving of benefit or favor, and eliciting some form of reciprocal return that is both voluntary and necessary for the continuation of the relationship*" (Barclay, *Paul and the Gift*, 575). In a more recent study, Barclay says "grace is free (unconditioned) but not cheap (without expectations or obligations)" (Barclay, *Paul and the Power of Grace*, 149). Noteworthy is that grace comes to us apart from our worth. A relationship with God is formed in that gift that transforms us into reciprocating agents who give to others. Which is exactly where Paul begins with his theme of generosity in our two chapters: Because God's grace given to us is so generous, we are to become agents of grace and gift. That is, generous.

We can call this a cycle of grace or cycle of giving. Phase one: Our loving God gives the gift of Christ to us. Phase two: We receive the gift of God's grace. Phase three: we respond with thanksgiving and responsive giving ourselves. Our relationship to God then is grace/gift-shaped.

ACCORDING TO ONE'S ABILITY

Each of us can give but each gives consistent with her ability. Paul, in verse three, says of the Macedonians that "they gave as much as they were able." In verse twelve Paul writes "the gift is acceptable according to what one has, not according to what one does not have." Very wise words, those. Comparing what one gives with what another person gives creates systemic unhealth in a church. Each is to give according to what one has. Even the tithe, which is never taught in the New Testament, can be very difficult for one family while for another a tithe is piddly. Paul seems here to replace the tithe in churches with proportional giving, or giving according to one's ability and income.

WILLINGLY

Some tension arises for one who reads carefully. Paul wants the Corinthians to give voluntarily or willingly, but he *wants* them to give, and he does not back down from either persuading them to give nor from comparing them to the Macedonians! So, I read his *willingly* statements with an eye on his larger vision for giving. "Entirely on their own, they urgently pleaded with us for the privilege of sharing" in participating in the collection for the poor in Jerusalem (8:3–4). He points to the "desire" of the Corinthians to give and of their "eager willingness" (8:11–12).

Coercion forms the opposite of willingness. Willingness respects both freedom and choice. Badgering, inspecting, bullying, intimidating, browbeating, reminding, guilt-producing words and behaviors are out of bounds if willingness prompts and shapes giving. Leaders need to trust people to make their own decisions.

The Collection

TERMS

Paul called his collection various terms, including a grace gift (1 Corinthians 16:3; 2 Corinthians 8:6), a blessing (9:5), a liturgy or a "public work's service" (9:12; *Second Testament*), a service (Romans 15:31; 1 Corinthians 16:15; 2 Corinthians 8:4), and a fellowship or "making resources common" (Romans 15:26; *Second Testament*). There is much to ponder in the use of such different terms. Each term explores how believers live together even when they disagree at times.

CHURCHES

Galatia (1 Corinthians 16:1)
Derbe, Lystra, Berea, Thessalonica (Acts 16:1; 20:4)
Macedonia (2 Corinthians 8:1–5; 9:2, 4)

Philippi (Acts 16:12, 16; 20:6)
Corinth (Romans 15:26)
Mysia, Ephesus (Acts 20:4)

THE POOR

This collection was for those who were poor. Christians inherited from their Jewish Bible and the practices of Judaism the use of their material resources for the good of the poor. In this they were distinguished from most of the Roman world where the poor languished and died or wrestled life from meager resources. If we factor in Galatians 2:10, Acts 11:27–30, Romans 15:26, and 2 Corinthians 8–9, there can be no doubt Paul's collection was for the poor, and the term for "poor" in this instance refers to the destitute driven to begging. Every Christian living consistently with the gospel, and we can see this especially in 2 Corinthians 8–9, generously contribute somehow to those in need. It is our inheritance as Bible-shaped believers. Paul urges that believers in Corinth, instead of cramming at the last minute, set aside money each week (1 Corinthians 16:2). The collection would be taken to Jerusalem. With Paul, at least in his plans, would be representatives from each church who would be accompanied with hearty letters of affirmation by Paul himself (16:3).

Scot McKnight, EBS: *1 Corinthians*, pp. 230–231

VIRTUOUS

Virtuous giving flows directly out of surrendering our lives (and resources) to God, and that is why Paul says the

Macedonians "gave themselves first of all to the Lord" and only then "to us" (8:5). That's the cycle of grace, phase two and three with phase one assumed. Paul ties grace-based giving to a life of virtue. Those marked by "faith" and "speech" and "knowledge" and "complete earnestness" and "love" for Paul's crew of missioners, will become agents of generosity (8:7). Generosity is a spiritual virtue for Paul, a witness to the power of God's grace at work in us.

ENCOURAGERS WELCOME

Above we joined Paul in frowning at coercion, but that does not exclude—let's call it "encouragement." Notice Paul has sent Titus to Corinth, and one suspects he's talking about the visit with the Severe Letter (Letter D). Paul encourages Titus to encourage the Corinthians to donate to the Collection, and to complete their good beginning of collecting funds (8:6). They had started but seem to have flagged in their giving. His next words are more an act of persuasion: "I am not commanding you, but I want to test the sincerity of your love by comparing it with the earnestness of others" (8:8). Two comments: when you say you are not ordering someone, even if you add that you could if you wanted to, you effectively put them on notice of an order. Furthermore, when you compare the Corinthians (Achaia) with the northern Greece churches (Macedonia), you are putting competitive pressure on the Corinthians. Has Paul crossed the line beyond willingness here?

EQUALITY

One of the most potent paragraphs about money in the entire Bible can be found at verses thirteen to fifteen. One word matters and one event matters. The word is *equality*, and it means just that, but the *event* defines what equality means. Equality assumes inequality or the term would not be needed. Christians inherited from Judaism a concern for the poor in a world where injustices and inequality reigned. Money matters and money has the power to harden hearts and stiffen the hands that give. Grace, once embraced deeply, softens hearts and opens the hands and turns believers into agents of generosity—toward equality with a big eye focused on the poor and marginalized and disadvantaged in our churches and societies. Systemic poverty must be recognized for the evil it is. The only solution to systemic poverty, or generational poverty, is to attack the system and revolutionize the system from the bottom up. Generational poverty deserves the Christian alternative of generational flourishing.

The event was the divine *manna* provisions for the children of Israel while in the wilderness (Exodus 16). God's formula for provisions was simple: enough for everyone, no less, no more. Here is what Exodus 16:18 says: "And when they measured it by the omer, the one who gathered much did not have too much, and the one who gathered little did not have too little. Everyone had gathered just as much as they needed." Equality is when everyone has what they need. When everyone helps those in need. The manna event defines equality: the apostle expects the Corinthians to be generous for others and still have what they need, and he expects the poor of Jerusalem to have what they need. And he expects that someday, if the Corinthians go low and the Jerusalem saints have an abundance, that they will reciprocate in this new covenant cycle of grace and generosity.

Paul's words, of course, are about believers in Corinth and Macedonians helping believers in Jerusalem. But the principles in the cycle of grace transform humans into the virtue of being generous so much that Christians become agents of generosity not only toward churches and other Christians but in society as well. The New Testament at times speaks of "doing good" with the sense of social acts of benevolence (cf. Matthew 5:16; Luke 6:9, 33, 35; 1 Timothy 6:18; 1 Peter 2:14, 15, 20; 3:17; 4:19; 3 John 11).

Judy Diehl rightly observes that "Christianity is expensive" in the sense that "it takes a lot of money to do God's will on earth. We note all of the good, godly organizations that need financial support: pastors, missionaries, churches, schools, and hospitals, just to name a few" (Diehl, *2 Corinthians*, 288). She's right. We have experienced God's good and abundant grace, and God's relationship of grace is transforming us into agents of generosity who are beyond worthy of its expensiveness!

QUESTIONS FOR REFLECTION AND APPLICATION

1. What is the starting point for Christian generosity?

2. How does Paul see giving and grace interacting?

3. How does the cycle of grace work?

4. What is your approach to giving?

5. How did you form your giving principles?

FOR FURTHER READING

John M.G. Barclay, *Paul and the Gift* (Grand
Rapids: Wm. B. Eerdmans, 2015).
John M.G. Barclay, *Paul and the Power of Grace*
(Grand Rapids: Wm. B. Eerdmans, 2020).
John Wesley, "The Use of Money," at chrome
-extension://efaidnbmnnnibpcajpcglclefindmkaj
/https://s3.us-east-1.amazonaws.com/gbod
-assets/generic/Use-Of-Money.pdf
Scot McKnight, Everyday Bible Study: *1 Corinthians*,
(Grand Rapids: HarperChristian Resources).

AMBASSADORS OF
THE COLLECTION

2 Corinthians 8:16–9:5

¹⁶ Thanks be to God, who put into the heart of Titus the same con-cern I have for you. ¹⁷ For Titus not only welcomed our appeal, but he is coming to you with much enthusiasm and on his own initiative. ¹⁸ And we are sending along with him the brother who is praised by all the churches for his service to the gospel. ¹⁹ What is more, he was chosen by the churches to accompany us as we carry the offering, which we administer in order to honor the Lord himself and to show our eagerness to help. ²⁰ We want to avoid any criticism of the way we administer this liberal gift. ²¹ For we are taking pains to do what is right, not only in the eyes of the Lord but also in the eyes of man.

²² In addition, we are sending with them our brother who has often proved to us in many ways that he is zealous, and now even more so because of his great confidence in you. ²³ As for Titus, he is my partner and co-worker among you; as for our brothers, they are representatives of the churches and an honor to Christ. ²⁴ Therefore show these men the proof of your love and the reason for our pride in you, so that the churches can see it.

^{9:1} There is no need for me to write to you about this service to the Lord's people. ² For I know your eagerness to help, and I have been boasting about it to the Macedonians, telling them that since

last year you in Achaia were ready to give; and your enthusiasm has stirred most of them to action. ³ But I am sending the brothers in order that our boasting about you in this matter should not prove hollow, but that you may be ready, as I said you would be. ⁴ For if any Macedonians come with me and find you unprepared, we—not to say anything about you—would be ashamed of having been so confident. ⁵ So I thought it necessary to urge the brothers to visit you in advance and finish the arrangements for the generous gift you had promised. Then it will be ready as a generous gift, not as one grudgingly given.

In the middle of all this tension between the Corinthians and Paul, the apostle stands up for the poor believers in Jerusalem by requesting funds from the Corinthians that will be sent to Jerusalem (8:19). I'm inclined to think Paul was confident Titus and others could win the Corinthians over to a warm relation with Paul and his coworkers. Their generosity would be the indicator of their warming up to Paul. Still, raising funds from them was a particular challenge. In fact, it has always been difficult, but persuading folks who don't like you seems next to impossible. We might need to pause to consider such a context for 2 Corinthians 8–9.

Paul's plan, remember, is to go north from Ephesus to Troas and then by boat or by land to Macedonia. Then he would return to Corinth in Achaia with the confidence the Corinthian collection would be in order for the trip to Jerusalem. He has sent Titus and two others as ambassadors to deliver pastoral care and to urge the Corinthians to get their funds ready. Titus was chosen for a reason.

AMBASSADORS

Instead of returning yet again to Corinth (Plan C, p. 36), Paul sent Titus and two brothers (8:18, 22) with instructions, as mentioned in today's passage, to meet up with him in Troas. We know Titus (see Sidebar on pp. 104) but we are not sure of the other two. One is called "the brother who is praised by all the churches for his service to the gospel" (8:18). Furthermore, this brother was selected by other churches to accompany Paul to Jerusalem (8.19). It appears this brother adds integrity and transparency to the collection. The next "brother" is known for being "zealous" or "serious" (McKnight, *Second Testament*) as well as for his "great confidence in you" (8:22). Many names have been suggested for the brothers, including Luke. It's fun to guess, especially if we know we are guessing. What is not fun to guess about is that Paul was deeply criticized by the Corinthians about his choice regarding from whom he would receive support for his ministry (8:20; 11:8–12; see Introduction, pp. 1–11; and 1 Corinthians 9:12, 15, 18). He did not accept funds from the Corinthians for his own ministry.

The reasons for sending the ambassadors and planning for them to go with him to Jerusalem are: (1) they want to honor the Lord in all they do (8:19), (2) they want to help the poor (8:19), (3) they want to "avoid any criticism" (8:20), (4) they want to do what is right in the eyes of God and man (8:21), and perhaps most of all (5) they want representatives from as many churches as possible to arrive in Jerusalem to show the believers there that the mission churches of Paul stand with the mother church. Perhaps, too, there was a concern for the safety of the funds. They were, after all, probably toting a large sum of money.

The Life of Titus

Titus is unmentioned in the book of Acts and, because he was a gentile, uncircumcised (Galatians 2:3). He rose rapidly into a church leader and was with Paul in that early mission for the poor (2:1, 10). We hear nothing about him until the third mission trip and the collection for the saints in Jerusalem. In the New Testament he is mentioned in Crete, Nicopolis, and Dalmatia (e.g., 2 Timothy 4:10).

In that early visit to Jerusalem, he visibly experienced an attempt for unity in the missions of Paul and Peter (Galatians 2:9). He becomes Paul's Ephesus-base ambassador of reconciliation with the Corinthian house churches. He was a partner in the gospel mission, which involved raising money (2 Corinthians 8:23), and he was the courier of the Severe Letter between Paul and Corinth. He was an agent, along with two others, in urging the Corinthians to ready their funds for Paul's trip to Jerusalem (8–9; cf. 2:12–17 and 7:12–23). In all this Paul knew Titus's obvious empathy in pastoral care (cf. 7:15).

Adapted from Scot McKnight, *The Pastoral Epistles*,
New Cambridge Bible Commentary, pp.14–15.

PREPARATION

So, Paul urges them to listen to the three brothers in this mission and get their funds ready (see 1 Corinthians 16:1–4).

The Corinthians were, at least in the past, all-in when it came to supporting the poor in Jerusalem: they were eager and ready to give (2 Corinthians 9:2).

Paul puts on his hat of persuasion again. In 8:24 he urges them to complete their collection as "proof of your love" and to show that his "pride" and "boasting" are not hollow. Two more expressions appear: if they are not ready when the brothers arrive, Paul will be "ashamed" and they would be failing in their promise (9:4, 5). He knows the Corinthians are capable of a "generous gift" that would not be "grudgingly given" (9:5), which means they chose to participate with enthusiasm (cf. 8:2–3, 11).

PRINCIPLES

I mention briefly both the repetition of principles already enunciated in the previous passage (8:1–15) but also the fresh ones: (1) Paul needs well-chosen coworkers at times. They are pragmatically chosen since he did not have time for yet another trip to Corinth. And they are also chosen because Paul probably thought he needed a reconciling voice like Titus's. (2) Any donations and public communications about funds require transparency because what happens with folks' money matters much. (3) Not only does the handing of funds require transparency, but all such matters either bring honor or disrepute to Christ himself (8:21, 23). (4) Affirmations of donors are both needed and need sensitivity. The aim is not to bolster their ego and fame but to affirm their commitment to the mission of the gospel and the relief of those in need. (5) Communications about donors can be a contagion of benevolence (9:2: "your enthusiasm has stirred most of them to action"). (6) Planning and adequate time for preparation give the donors time to pray, ponder, and prepare their gifts. (7) Avoid gimmicks and tricks.

Remember this: Paul's theory of proportional giving, which is the Christian replacement of the tithe, embodies a theology of God's grace to us, exhibited in Christ himself, and that grace given transforms us into agents of benevolence and grace toward others.

QUESTIONS FOR REFLECTION AND APPLICATION

1. What is Paul's plan for collecting funds for believers in Jerusalem?

2. How does Paul use persuasion to bring about this financial gift?

3. What role does Titus play in the collection?

4. Do you tend to practice tithing, or do you tend toward proportional giving?

5. Have you ever received generous giving from another Christian? How did that gift make a difference in your life?

FOR FURTHER READING

Scot McKnight, *The Pastoral Epistles*, New Cambridge Bible Commentary (New York: Cambridge University Press, 2023).

PRINCIPLES IN THE CYCLE OF GRACE (2)

2 Corinthians 9:6–15

⁶ *Remember this: Whoever sows sparingly will also reap sparingly, and whoever sows generously will also reap generously.* ⁷ *Each of you should give what you have decided in your heart to give, not reluctantly or under compulsion, for God loves a cheerful giver.* ⁸ *And God is able to bless you abundantly, so that in all things at all times, having all that you need, you will abound in every good work.* ⁹ *As it is written:*

> *"They have freely scattered their gifts to the poor;*
> *their righteousness endures forever."*

¹⁰ *Now he who supplies seed to the sower and bread for food will also supply and increase your store of seed and will enlarge the harvest of your righteousness.* ¹¹ *You will be enriched in every way so that you can be generous on every occasion, and through us your generosity will result in thanksgiving to God.*

¹² *This service that you perform is not only supplying the needs of the Lord's people but is also overflowing in many expressions of thanks to God.* ¹³ *Because of the service by which you have proved yourselves, others will praise God for the obedience that*

*accompanies your confession of the gospel of Christ, and for your
generosity in sharing with them and with everyone else. [14] And in
their prayers for you their hearts will go out to you, because of the
surpassing grace God has given you. [15] Thanks be to God for his
indescribable gift!*

Churches still need to be instructed to support Christian
ministries. Many in the USA can neither define "enough"
nor do they have a gospel-shaped theory of investments. I just
reworked David de Silva's words in the previous two sen-
tences. In a sermon he preached about the diverse investments
of a church's manifold gifts and ministries: from missions to
compassion to pastoral staff to musicians to buildings and to
the spiritual awakening and formation of our youth (de Silva,
In Season and Out, 190–198). Over the years an entire quiver
full of arrows have been used to pierce through the grip
church folks have on their money. Some of these arrows have
been needed; others have been coercive, manipulative, and
plain trickery. In today's passage, we hear four more principles, added to the six in 8:1–15, at work in the cycle of grace.
Here again are the three phases of the cycle of grace.

> Phase one: Our loving God gives the gift of Christ
>   to us.
> Phase two: We receive the gift of God's grace.
> Phase three: We respond with thanksgiving and
>   responsive giving ourselves.

Our relationship to God then is grace/gift-shaped. The
last verse of today's passage expresses the cycle of grace:
"Thanks be to God for his indescribable gift!" (9:15). In fact,
the word translated in the NIV with "thanks" is actually the
same word for grace. So, "Grace to God for his unexplainable
gift" (McKnight, *Second Testament*).

PROPORTIONAL GIVING, PROPORTIONAL BLESSING

One trick used by those who want church folks to give is to promise what givers will get. We must be careful. Yet, we need to be careful twice: there is more than enough evidence in Deuteronomy 28 to know that God blesses the obedient, and there is more than enough evidence in Job and in the life of Jesus, to factor in that the obedient can be persecuted. Blessings can be delayed, with the ultimate blessing being eternal life in the presence of a loving God. But the correlation of behavior and effects flows throughout the Bible (cf. Luke 6:38; Galatians 6:7–9).

Paul calls people to give in a way consistent with what they have (2 Corinthians 8:3, 11). If some give "sparingly," that is less than they must give, their blessings will be sparing, while those who give "generously" will experience generous-er blessings (9:6). Generous giving is shaped by personal choice: "what you have decided in your heart to give" (9:7). God wants a "gleeful giver," and frowns on giving "out of pain or out of necessity" (9:7; *Second Testament*). David de Silva, continuing his thoughts about diversifying our investments in the kingdom of God, paraphrases these verses well: "The one who throws only a little into these investments will only enjoy a small return, but the one who invests heavily in these ventures will have a whopping return. But you can invest whatever you decide to invest—it's up to you . . . For God loves a cheerful investor" (de Silva, *In Season and Out*, 196). Leaders then are warned here not to coerce or cajole or make giving a billed debt and payment.

Beware of being promised or promising that there is an absolute correlation between proportional giving and proportional blessings. We may need to be learning something more or other than blessings in return for donations. Leaders need to trust each person to do what Paul says here: let each person decide in her heart what to give (8:7).

DIVINE ABUNDANCE

Perhaps the true blessing of heart-felt giving is that "you will abound in every good work" (9:8). Knowing scriptures as he does, Paul's statement either leads him to Psalm 112:9 (quoted at 2 Corinthians 9:9), or that verse in the book of Psalms generated his reframing of it into some wisdom. Take your pick. Those who know the Bible often don't even know they are reframing the Bible! What Paul is getting at is a "harvest of righteousness" and be "enriched in every way" and be able to be "generous" (9:10). Again, we must be cautious in overpromising without ignoring the tangible blessings so many experience. My experience with faithful givers to the Lord's work is a tranquil satisfaction with what the Lord has done in them over the years of their giving.

GOD RECEIVES THE THANKS

Paul cuts the feet and legs off the statues so popular in Corinth and other Rome-based cities. They all had statues all over the cities honoring the donors and benefactors. Paul says the Corinthians' gifts will result, not in their being honored, but in thanks to God (9:12–13). We return to the cycle of grace. The reason God is thanked is not because someone is humble or even pretends to be humble about their generosity. No, it is because it all begins with the grace-gift of God named Jesus who, through the Spirit, transforms us into agents of grace. Our grace-gifts are but the outworking of God's own work in us.

LOVING RELATIONSHIPS

The ever-vulnerable and emotion-shaped Paul turns it up in 9:14. Read this carefully: "And in their prayers for you *their hearts will go out to you*" and they will do this because of their own experience of God's cycle of grace: "because of the surpassing grace God has given you." The NIV has added the word "hearts" to an expression that can be translated "their longing" and even "their missing or wanting you, or their yearning for you." One of the benefits of donations in the Lord's ministry is relationships with other believers with similar passions. Grace unites people into siblings who love and long to be with one another. Giving has the capacity at times to create that sensibility, that desire to be with others, that desire to express thanks and that desire to be thanked (for God's sake).

I have not said anything about this, but I find it believable, though not easily proven, that 2 Corinthians 8–9 could be an earlier communication from Paul to the Corinthians that has been spliced onto the end of the story about Paul and Titus we read about in chapters one through seven. I only write this because chapter ten, like chapter eight, takes us into new territory.

QUESTIONS FOR REFLECTION AND APPLICATION

1. What freedom does Paul give to believers to determine what they will give?

2. What is the balance between encouraging people to give knowing God will bless them and not over-promising?

3. How is God glorified in our giving?

4. Have you ever been promised certain outcomes by ministry leaders if you were to give to them? Did those promised blessings materialize for you?

5. Has your giving ever resulted in better sibling relationships with other believers?

FOR FURTHER READING

David de Silva, *In Season and Out* (Bellingham, Washington: Lexham, 2019).

THE CORINTHIAN COMPLAINT CULTURE

2 Corinthians 10:1–18

[1] *By the humility and gentleness of Christ, I appeal to you—*

TIMIDITY

[Complaint] I, Paul, who am "timid" when face to face with you, but "bold" toward you when away!

[Response] [2] I beg you that when I come I may not have to be as bold as I expect to be toward some people who think that we live by the standards of this world. [3] For though we live in the world, we do not wage war as the world does. [4] The weapons we fight with are not the weapons of the world. On the contrary, they have divine power to demolish strongholds. [5] We demolish arguments and every pretension that sets itself up against the knowledge of God, and we take captive every thought to make it obedient to Christ. [6] And we will be ready to punish every act of disobedience, once your obedience is complete.

CONSIDER THE PERSON

[7] [Complaint] You are judging by appearances [Look at matters in the face!]

[Response] If anyone is confident that they belong to Christ, they should consider again that we belong to Christ just as much as they do.

BOASTING ABOUT MINISTRY AUTHORITY

[Complaint] [8] So even if I boast somewhat freely about the authority the Lord gave us for building you up rather than tearing you down, I will not be ashamed of it.

[Response] [9] I do not want to seem to be trying to frighten you with my letters. [10] For some say, "His letters are weighty and forceful, but in person he is unimpressive and his speaking amounts to nothing." [11] Such people should realize that what we are in our letters when we are absent, we will be in our actions when we are present.

BOASTING ABOUT MINISTRY'S 'WHO DOES WHAT AND WHERE?'

[Complaint] [12] We do not dare to classify or compare ourselves with some who commend themselves. When they measure themselves by themselves and compare themselves with themselves, they are not wise.

[Response] [13] We, however, will not boast beyond proper limits, but will confine our boasting to the sphere of service God himself has assigned to us, a sphere that also includes you. [14] We are not going too far in our boasting, as would be the case if we had not

come to you, for we did get as far as you with the gospel of Christ.
[15] Neither do we go beyond our limits by boasting of work done
by others. Our hope is that, as your faith continues to grow, our
sphere of activity among you will greatly expand, [16] so that we can
preach the gospel in the regions beyond you. For we do not want to
boast about work already done in someone else's territory. [17] But,
"Let the one who boasts boast in the Lord." [18] For it is not the one
who commends himself who is approved, but the one whom the
Lord commends.

Special Note to the Reader: I have reformatted this passage into
Complaints and Responses.

Every leader in every church ever has experienced some
complaints. I recently read an article in *The Harvard
Business Review* entitled "4 Types of Employee Complaints—
and How to Respond" (URL at the end of this chapter).
You're curious about it, aren't you? I was, so I read it. The
authors, Alyson Meister and Nele Dael, both work in the
IMD Business School in Lausanne, Switzerland. Here are
the four types of complaints and complainers, with a brief
description of each:

1. Productive complainer: they want to help, and they
   can help.
2. Venters: vigorous, emotional complaining. Such persons want to express dissatisfaction and perhaps also
   to find some allies. There is a double burden on the
   institution: to receive and to deal with the person in
   his emotional outburst.
3. Chronic complainer: we probably know people with
   a constant gripe about someone or something. The
   authors observe that chronic complainers exhaust the
   energies, compassions, and relations with others. Yet,

117

they think, too, that chronic complainers, ever free to complain, can turn up important issues to consider. Commonly the chronic complainer begins to be ignored.

4. Malicious complainers: this person seeks to degrade and undermine others and to gain an advantage for themselves. The authors find the malicious complainer is out to gain some advantage. They "serve the self at the expense of others." The authors connect this person to gossip and backstabbing. "This type of complaining rarely has an upside—and it can create a toxic and psychologically unsafe" culture and it can "lower team morale." "Malicious complaining only creates personal gain that harms others and the collective, decreases productivity, and creates a toxic work environment."

If you want to have some fun, and if you can decide more or less to agree with Paul, you can go read 2 Corinthians 10–13 and mark in the columns of your Bible which number a given complaint (bracketed in the translation above) expresses. In general, however productive some of the criticisms of Paul may have been, Paul has been traumatized by the malicious complaints reverberating in Corinth. Chapters ten to thirteen reveal a Paul we barely, if ever, glimpse in his other letters. Here we encounter a full-on response, and much of it emotional and all of it resulting from the trauma of unjust accusations.

Responding to complaints determines the culture of the workplace. For the leader with the power to do something about complaints, dismissing, minimizing, or ignoring the complaints will damage trust in the leader. When the complaints are "unregulated," the complaints can produce "complaint contagion"—the culture becomes contaminated with negativity and at times will lead to "learned helplessness." Leaders need to be interested and curious and to facilitate constructive complaints. They also need to "tackle destructive complaints." If mediation does not help, support may be needed or even dismissed. Complainers need also to learn that their complaints may not lead to the results they want; if they persist in their complaints, they become toxic to the workplace culture. Sometimes leaders, and in our case the apostle Paul, must make decisions that do not conform to the chronic or malicious complainer's desires. At times leaders respond as long described by John Chrysostom, famous saint of the fourth and fifth centuries. His biographer describes Chrysostom's response to his critics in these words: "He also has to deal with constant attacks on himself, however unjustified and from whatever quarter they come, calmly and constructively," and quoting Chrysostom's own advice in dealing with the complainers, "forgiving irrational onslaughts, without making a fuss and losing his temper" (Kelly, *Golden Mouth*, 84). We are not sure Paul followed that kind of approach in every circumstance, and neither did Chrysostom!

Before we turn to the text, we must be careful to remember that the critic complaining about Paul thought he (the critic) was justified in doing so. The critic thought he was right; Paul thought the critic was wrong. The critic's words traveled around Corinth, and Paul's words have traveled to millennia to reach us. I don't believe Paul is always right in his self- and others-perceptions, but in my reflections on these chapters, I will give Paul the benefit of the doubt as a leader who became aware of allegations, accusations, and complaints. And responded, at times fiercely.

The complaints against Paul network with one another, but I think we can discern four separable complaints in today's passage.

STARTING POINT

Paul begins with words that reveal the *tone* of what is to follow. When responding to complainers, and these sure look like malicious complainers, leaders have always been tempted to lash out and retaliate. Paul wants the Corinthians to understand his emotional state and his voice level when he writes, "By the humility and gentleness of Christ, I appeal to you" (10:1). The terms have various translations, like "meekness and fairness" (McKnight, *Second Testament*) or "gentleness and kindness" (CEB). The transparent Paul does not say "in my anger" or "out of distress" and neither does he say, "I could pull out the apostle card." He has listened, and he responds in a manner that can only be called respectful and pastoral.

Titus probably read this letter to the Corinthians. Many have argued 2 Corinthians 10–13 is or reflects the Severe Letter (Letter D) and has been attached to chapters one through nine. Others believe fresh nasty news arrived from Corinth and 10–13 is a response. Whether fresh news from Titus or not, whether our chapters are the Severe Letter or not, the reader was instructed by Paul to convey the tone of 10:1 all the way through the end of the letter. That would have been a challenge for anyone who loved Paul and believed he had been wronged. We will all need to keep this in mind as we read on.

TIMIDITY

The complaint, as Paul has heard it, is "I, Paul, who am 'timid' when face to face with you, but 'bold' toward you when away!" (10:1). Take social media, where absence from others makes a Twitter-er (X-er) bolder. Or take comments on a blog or website. For almost twenty years I have been blogging, and early on I formed a principle for commenters:

Say only what you would say to someone if you were sitting with them over coffee in a café. Someone has called out Paul in his absence about his tone when absent! That is, when present he is fine; when absent he raises his voice. They accuse him of "timidity," a cardinal sin for a man in the Roman world. *Romanitas* formed men into confident, masculinist, and boastful males, especially in public. Paul, thus, didn't fit their ideal.

He responds with anti-*Romanitas*. He chooses not to operate "by the standards of this world" (10:2). The NIV's "world," however, translates a word that means "flesh" (McKnight, *Second Testament*), and flesh puts an important unredeemed edge to what he is saying. Their fleshy ways are not his ways, and if they can hear him out, he will not need to be "bold" when he arrives. Which is to say, he's not timid, he can be bold, but only when they act fleshly (10:2). His anti-flesh approach is to "demolish reasonings" and "high-status" claims to "capture" all things for "Christ-obedience" (10:4–5; *Second Testament*). He is not timid. He is bold, but only for Christ and not for his own status. God's kind of power operates through weakness, not brashness.

His response entails a threat: "And we will be ready to punish every act of disobedience, once your obedience is complete" (10:6). Which is to say, once I know you Corinthians have done what is right, then discipline will need to occur.

CONSIDER THE PERSON

The words of 10:7 hint, leaving us wondering. Is this an imperative? "Look at matters in the face!" (McKnight, *Second Testament*). Or is it a simple statement? "You are judging by appearances" (NIV). The Greek word can be read either way. Is Paul pleading with them to *Please just consider the facts about me*, or is he claiming they are judging by externalities?

Everywhere else Paul uses the term behind "Look!" it is an imperative, so I go with that. He is asking them to look at the complaints by pondering what he is like. What he has accomplished. What powers God did among them.

His response is such a personal appeal: *If anyone wants to consider themselves a follower of Jesus, that person ought to recognize I can make the same claim.* The words are general enough that specifics are unclear. Paul here claims his ministry cannot be discounted by those who think they are the special apostles of Christ. That is, he contends the group against him has no more claim than he does. In chapter eleven, we will see the complainers claim to be apostles as well as "servants of Christ" (11:13, 23).

To shift lanes just a bit, I use women pastors as an example. Men can make the claim that they are called to preach or pastor, and no one doubts the possibility. Women who make the same claims are challenged constantly with their calling. They must prove themselves daily. Instead of just pastoring or preaching, on them is laid the requirement to respond to those who question their calling. At times, women can join Paul and say, "Look at matters in the face!" Just look at her spiritual fruit, at the trust she has gained, just look at the formation she has led . . . evidence is hard to deny. Those who continue with the criticisms most likely fit the chronic or malicious complainers categories.

BOASTING ABOUT MINISTRY

The next complaint concerns two forms of boasting, beginning with their complaint that he is boasting about authority (10:8), to which Paul provides a response (10:9–11). They complain Paul boasted "somewhat freely" (or "excessively"; *Second Testament*) about (1) the authority given him by the Lord. They contend his authority was to build them up but not to tear them down (10:8). (2) His complainers repeat the timidity complaint as well, saying his letters convey a heavy authority tone while his presence is "unimpressive." Paul squeezes in yet another complaint here: (3) that his preaching "amounts to nothing" (10:10). In a world where public rhetoric and speeches were forms of entertainment and often available in Corinth, to contend Paul's preaching degraded speech itself was an assault on his giftedness. They degraded his ministry in order to build up their guy, whoever it was, and Apollos is the best guess. By the way, every Sunday the one preaching feels the potential of this criticism. (Those who don't, need to.)

He responds, first, that he is not one bit "ashamed" of boasting in his calling, whether it is "formation or demolition" (10:8; *Second Testament*). Second, he explains his intention: the Severe Letter was not designed to "frighten" (10:9). Third, he makes clear that the gravity of the letter will be matched by gravity when he arrives if that is what is needed (10:11). His response then claims to be full-orbed pastoral care, that his intentions are not negative, and that his behaviors are consistent. That he intends only to do what God wants him to do.

At this point, and we are only part way into this section of the letter, you may think *You are defending yourself too much, Paul*. I will guess for him in saying *This letter was needfully severe because of the behavior of some in Corinth*. He offers in these three chapters a point-by-point refutation of the complainers, which he thinks are malicious. There's a time to defend oneself and a time not to defend oneself. Paul chooses the former.

BOASTING ABOUT MINISTRY'S 'WHO DOES WHAT AND WHERE?'

Those with complaints against Paul somehow were comparing Paul's rival leaders with Paul. To the detriment of Paul (10:12).

The issues in the comparison no doubt are at work in these chapters, but they surely involved his public speaking skills, his use of money, his timidity and trickery, as well as his favoring of other churches. What was also part of their complaint was that Paul had exceeded the parameters and invaded the territory (parish-like) of others, and it seems they don't think Paul ought to have jurisdiction in Corinth (10:13–18).

His response winds around and in and through the complaints. First, he claims it is unwise for one circle of complainers to compare themselves with one another. Of course, they will come up with affirmations of one another (10:12). Second, he addresses the parish complaint. He contends he will "boast" about the "sphere of service God himself has assigned" to him (10:13), which means Achaia, including Corinth (10:13–14). His claim is *we got to you first* (Martin, *2 Corinthians*, 505). Third, he does not boast about other parishes because they are not assigned to him (10:15, 16b). Fourth, he expresses hope that his ministry among them will expand territorially (10:15–16). Finally, he turns it all back to God: all boasting ultimately needs to be boasting about God's work among us. All commendations, too, need to be God's commendations (10:17–18).

COMPLAINT CULTURE

The opponents of Paul somehow got the upper hand in Corinth. Or at least they thought they did. They verbally degraded Paul to lift themselves above him as the true spiritual leader of Corinth. Their approach was to form a coalition of those who agree with them, which Paul saw as an abscess of the flesh's way in this world. Paul's sensitivity, backed up with a cross-shaped approach to ministry, made him an easy target. Plus, he wasn't around so the rumors about him swirled into believable truths.

THE CORINTHIAN COMPLAINT CULTURE

Paul's a wounded, traumatized apostle. The complainers' criticisms have stung him. We are reading a letter in which we hear his representations of his complainers. They are enough for any sympathetic reader at least to hear a deeply wounded man. We may wonder if his responses are the best way to go, but at least he is communicating his heart with them. An honest heart is a good place to start. We may need to return to 10:1 again, which informs us of Paul's tone in all the above: "By the humility and gentleness of Christ, I appeal to you." Paul's approach was to take on the complaints directly and even forcefully, but I do believe we can approach them more accurately if we take 10:1 into close consideration.

Questions for Reflection and Application

1. Using the categories from the *Harvard Business Review* article about complainers, identify the types of complaints Paul is dealing with. What do you find?

2. How do complaints affect cultures?

3. What is your impression of Paul's responses to his critics so far?

4. Who has been a good example to you of responding to complaints and complainers with the "humility and gentleness of Christ"?

5. Think of a situation where you needed to defend yourself or where you thought someone else needed to be defended. What does defending oneself in a situation like Paul's accomplish?

J.N.D. Kelly, *Golden Mouth: The Story of John Chrysostom—Ascetic, Preacher, Bishop* (Grand Rapids: Wm. B. Eerdmans, 1995).
Alyson Meister and Nele Dael, "4 Types of Employee Complaints—and How to Respond," in *The Harvard Business Review*: https://hbr.org /2023/05/4-types-of-employee-complaints-and -how-to-respond

THE LEADING
COMPLAINERS

2 Corinthians 11:1–15

[1] I hope you will put up with me in a little foolishness. Yes, please put up with me! [2] I am jealous for you with a godly jealousy. I promised you to one husband, to Christ, so that I might present you as a pure virgin to him. [3] But I am afraid that just as Eve was deceived by the serpent's cunning, your minds may somehow be led astray from your sincere and pure devotion to Christ. [4] For if someone comes to you and preaches a Jesus other than the Jesus we preached, or if you receive a different spirit from the Spirit you received, or a different gospel from the one you accepted, you put up with it easily enough.

[5] I do not think I am in the least inferior to those "super-apostles." [6] I may indeed be untrained as a speaker, but I do have knowledge. We have made this perfectly clear to you in every way. [7] Was it a sin for me to lower myself in order to elevate you by preaching the gospel of God to you free of charge? [8] I robbed other churches by receiving support from them so as to serve you. [9] And when I was with you and needed something, I was not a burden to anyone, for the brothers who came from Macedonia supplied what I needed. I have kept myself from being a burden to you in any way, and will continue to do so. [10] As surely as the truth of Christ is in

me, nobody in the regions of Achaia will stop this boasting of mine.
¹¹ Why? Because I do not love you? God knows I do!

¹² And I will keep on doing what I am doing in order to cut the
ground from under those who want an opportunity to be considered
equal with us in the things they boast about. ¹³ For such people
are false apostles, deceitful workers, masquerading as apostles of
Christ. ¹⁴ And no wonder, for Satan himself masquerades as an
angel of light. ¹⁵ It is not surprising, then, if his servants also mas-
querade as servants of righteousness. Their end will be what their
actions deserve.

Sometimes you have to tell the truth directly to get the
attention of the complainer. Or perhaps to jar the complainer from his or her self-confident complaints. Complainers
at the center of a complaint culture think they are right and
the one they criticize is wrong. And, to complete the loop,
the one thought to be wrong thinks he or she is right, too!
The complainer will find others who support him, and he
may even trumpet their support as proof of his being the
one in the right. It may take an independent investigation to
come to terms. My experience is that the results of an investigator, no matter how independent or how well done, are
rejected by the one who thinks the results should have gone
in their favor instead. There is no independent investigator
with Paul. So, he steps into the middle of this culture with
his own responses.

Sometimes you speak out of your trauma. Trauma
"involves an event that overwhelms the normal human
capacity to adapt or cope" (Singer, "Toward a More Trauma-
Informed Church"). Paul's trauma was caused by perceived
false accusations and perceived interpersonal betrayal and
degradation of his integrity and status. Through Titus,
Paul spoke to the Corinthians out of his own trauma. Very
few pastors, the fortunate ones excepted, have not been

traumatized at some level by the congregants or by their board. Since pastors and leaders are often criticized in our culture, I want to focus here on the trauma caused to church leaders by others, including the congregation. (This does not dismiss the important fact that some pastors have preyed upon and traumatized their congregants, but those are not the situations we have in mind here.)

The symptoms of relational trauma include a disorientation of what is real, intruding thoughts and memories of the breakdown of the relationship, a numbing of relational freedom and feelings, and a sense of hyper-attentiveness to possible signs of relational danger. Those who have experienced relational trauma often go through three responses: revelation, response, and reorientation. Eagle's Wing Counseling defines relational trauma responses in this way (see link below; used with permission). This list is about marriage relationship trauma, but the same responses also apply to other types of relationships.

> **Revelation**: "This stage is marked with shock and catastrophic loss of emotional safety and trust as the betrayed spouse finds out/attempts to find out the full scope of the traumatic behaviors. Betrayed spouses are flooded with questions and want answers to the who, what, when, where, why, and how of the situation. Betrayed spouses can feel 'frantic' trying to assess the truth of the situation."
>
> **Response**: "This is when the Reality Disorientation is at its peak. All of the physical and psychological symptoms are at their most intense. These include, but are not limited to, anger, grief, depression, anxiety, bargaining, avoidance, and confusion. There can be extreme mood swings from intense anger to severe depression/numbness/confusion. This stage is also

marked by continued collection and verification of evidence, deciding if the relationship will continue, evaluating the [other person's] . . . response to the trauma, beginning to set boundaries and/or consequences, dealing with trauma triggers, questioning what the future holds, seeking treatment, and deciding whom to tell."

Reorientation: "This stage is marked by an acceptance of the situation, symptoms becoming more manageable, engaging in personal healing work from the trauma, integrating the past, present, and future reality, restoring trust and safety with God, self, and others."

No one can say for sure what Paul experienced, but a slow reading of 2 Corinthians 10–13 reveals Paul's sensitivity and signs of relational trauma. How he responded to the various, at times brutal, criticisms can be instructive for us. At the least, they provide opportunities for us to ponder how to respond when relational breakdown and trauma occur. In our day, we would say Paul needed a therapist.

PERSONAL PASTORING

Paul goes personal again to open today's passage (11:1–4). Seven times Paul uses the term fool/foolishness for this letter of defense (11:1, 16, 17, 19, 21; 12:6, 11). Surely the leading complainers have traumatizingly called Paul a fool, so he turns the term upside down by embracing it for himself. That would be just like Paul. His self-defense, boasting, and comparison with others, which he did not permit for the complainers (10:12), is an act of foolishness to which these complainers have driven him. Here is how Paul explains his foolishness: first, he believes his boasting is a humble form of boasting, and (2) that his boasting, which looks foolish even to him, is driven to bring glory to God and not to himself.

His personal foolishness then morphs into a relational appeal. The NIV uses the English term "jealousy," but this term, used so often for envy rather than the personal desire for status recognition, misses what Paul is saying. I prefer the term "zeal" (11:2; *Second Testament*). Paul was zealous for the Corinthians to be restored to Christ and to himself. He likens his zealous passion for them to a faithful marital relationship (11:2). Thinking of marriage, he quickly turns to Genesis 1–3. He fears they will be deceived from their faithfulness as Eve was deceived in Eden (11:3). A traumatized person often connects situations to past trauma, which Paul does in 11:4. Paul points to someone's arrival in Corinth who distorted the "Jesus we preached" and the "Spirit you received" (11:4). The problem is their lack of discernment of the corrupted gospel at work in the leading complainers.

More signs of his trauma come to the surface in the next two observations: Paul's personal pastoral relationship with the Corinthians now shifts, rather dramatically, to buzzword descriptions of their complaints against Paul as well as to a direct critique accompanied by some self-defense.

Traumatized Paul

Paul's speech about the complainers and his self-defense are signs of being traumatized. He may not recognize the term, but he knows trauma by experience.

Pete Singer, a specialist in trauma, says "Trauma involves an event that overwhelms the normal human capacity to adapt or cope" (p. 3 of Singer's manuscript).

A more complex understanding comes from SAMHSA:

Trauma "results from an event, series of events, or set of circumstances that is experienced by an individual as physically or emotionally harmful or life threatening, and that has lasting effects on the person's functioning and mental, physical, social, emotional, or spiritual well-being."

SOME MORE
COMPLAINTS DESCRIBED

Paul passes on what appears to be complaints by the leading complainers, whom he derisively calls "super-apostles," and probably because they may have been called that by their followers (11:5). They mirrored so much of what Paul himself had done. They see him as "inferior" and "untrained as a speaker" and that he has "lowered" himself and preached to them "free of charge" and that he therefore "robbed" other churches when ministering to them (11:5–8). He adds a few verses down that these leading complainers searched for "an opportunity to be considered equal with" Paul and his coworkers and thus had some "boast" themselves (11:12). These all have to do with the status of a community's teacher, and competition for status recognition drove much of the energy in Corinth. Paul shunned their support because he did not take support from churches until they had matured into self-sufficiency. The super apostles probably did take support. The community's status rose when it could say it supported its own teachers. Paul's refusal of their support shamed the Corinthians most concerned with public status.

Parallels between Paul and the Leading Complainers

Paul	Complainers
Jewish	Jewish (11:22)
Minister	Ministers (6:3, 11:23)
Apostle	Apostles (1:1, 11:5, 13)
Preaches gospel	Preach the gospel (10:14, 11:4)
Preaches Jesus	Preach Jesus (4:5, 11:4)

Adapted from Paul Barnett, *Paul: A Pastor's Heart in Second Corinthians*, p. 37.

SOME MORE SELF-DEFENSE

The leading complainers think Paul is "inferior"; Paul denies that. They think he is "untrained"; he says, "I do have knowledge." They preach a different gospel; he preaches the gospel about Jesus Christ. They think he shamed them by refusing support; he thinks he elevated them by ministering "free of charge"; they think he "robbed other churches" by taking support from them while ministering in Corinth; he thinks he did not "burden" them at all (11:4–10). And he does this because he loves them, and God knows full well Paul does love them (11:11).

This *they* followed by a *he* back-and-forth reveals the pain at work in Paul. The pain turns next into labeling and even lashing out.

LABELING

Paul partly turned over their complaints when he ironically called them "super-apostles" (11:5). But he ratchets the labels up when he calls them "false apostles, deceitful workers" who are "masquerading as apostles of Christ"—and connects that with Satan! (11:13). He knows the judgment of God awaits them when "their end will be what their actions deserve" (11:15). Labels were one of the most common forms of public debate in the ancient world, and his labeling of the complainers (my label!) makes me wonder if Paul has transgressed his "humility and gentleness of Christ" approach in 10:1. Yet, does not a sympathetic reading of these passages elicit some sympathy for Paul for how traumatized he was by the Corinthians?

Politicians and preachers, on social media or not, still label others in order to create boundaries between themselves and their opponents, and to provide those who are inside that boundary with them to identify themselves. Labels discredit the other as deviant. A labeler uses terms to build up his own status and to warn those with the labeler of the danger of the other. Labels reveal far more about a relationship between two people or two groups than they do about the objective realities of the persons or the groups. Labeling should not be assigned to pure evil. The human mind makes meaning and organizes society through classifying. To be in a group means not to be in another group. Group identity, like kingdom coalition, requires an over-against-ness. Or, "in" requires an "out." Labeling becomes a vice when designed to degrade another person, and at that point it joins hands with the malicious complainer. So, "be careful little tongue what you say."

QUESTIONS FOR REFLECTION AND APPLICATION

1. How might have the Corinthians' treatment of Paul traumatized him?

2. Do you think Paul's foolishness and his defense of himself in these passages are ironical? That is, is the surface appearance of boasting perhaps mocking their boasting, and not real boasting?

3. What do you think of the idea that "Paul needed a therapist"?

4. How have you seen labeling work to create "in" groups and "out" groups?

5. Have you ever experienced relational trauma? If so, which of the responses listed in this section did you go through?

FOR FURTHER READING

Eagle's Wing Counseling: https://www.eagleswings counseling.com/relational-trauma-response
For another study: https://psychcentral.com/ptsd /what-is-relational-trauma#signs-and-symptoms
Paul Barnett, *Paul: A Pastor's Heart in Second Corinthians* (Sydney, Australia: Aquila, 2012).
Pete Singer, "Toward a More Trauma-Informed Church: Equipping Faith Communities to Prevent and Respond to Abuse," in *Currents in Theology and Mission,* forthcoming 2024.
Substance Abuse and Mental Health Services Administration. SAMHSA's Concept of Trauma and Guidance for a Trauma-Informed Approach. HHS publication number (SMA). Rockville, MD: Substance Abuse and Mental Health Services Administration, 2014.

TURNING BOASTING
UPSIDE DOWN

2 Corinthians 11:16–33

[16] I repeat: Let no one take me for a fool. But if you do, then tolerate me just as you would a fool, so that I may do a little boasting. [17] In this self-confident boasting I am not talking as the Lord would, but as a fool. [18] Since many are boasting in the way the world does, I too will boast. [19] You gladly put up with fools since you are so wise! [20] In fact, you even put up with anyone who enslaves you or exploits you or takes advantage of you or puts on airs or slaps you in the face. [21] To my shame I admit that we were too weak for that!

Whatever anyone else dares to boast about—I am speaking as a fool—I also dare to boast about. [22] Are they Hebrews? So am I. Are they Israelites? So am I. Are they Abraham's descendants? So am I. [23] Are they servants of Christ? (I am out of my mind to talk like this.) I am more. I have worked much harder, been in prison more frequently, been flogged more severely, and been exposed to death again and again. [24] Five times I received from the Jews the forty lashes minus one. [25] Three times I was beaten with rods, once I was pelted with stones, three times I was shipwrecked, I spent a night and a day in the open sea, [26] I have been constantly on the move. I have been in danger from rivers, in danger from bandits, in danger from my fellow Jews, in danger from Gentiles; in danger in the city, in danger in the country, in danger at sea; and in danger from false believers. ²⁷ I have labored and toiled and have often gone without sleep; I have known hunger and thirst and have often gone without food; I have been cold and naked. ²⁸ Besides everything else, I face daily the pressure of my concern for all the churches. ²⁹ Who is weak, and I do not feel weak? Who is led into sin, and I do not inwardly burn?

³⁰ If I must boast, I will boast of the things that show my weakness. ³¹ The God and Father of the Lord Jesus, who is to be praised forever, knows that I am not lying. ³² In Damascus the governor under King Aretas had the city of the Damascenes guarded in order to arrest me. ³³ But I was lowered in a basket from a window in the wall and slipped through his hands.

I begin with a long quotation from Philip Plyming, whose own suffering of abuse provided a lens for rethinking Paul. What you just read in today's passage forms the heart of Plyming's lessons learned. The heart of Plyming's message is that we cannot expect blessings on top of blessings, or victories on top of victories. Life deals hard breaks, but opposition to the gospel deals them, too. Paul suffered more than most, but his posture toward suffering was revolutionized by his theology of the cross. Paul did not relish persecution; he had no suffering-is-good-for-ya complex. No. Paul suffered. He looked suffering in the face. He coped with suffering by reframing it through the cross, and Plyming has done the same with the following principal lessons:

> I've learned that it was because of specific values within the Corinthian church that Paul chose to foreground his own hardship in the way he did. The Corinthian church had a culture problem—and it is a problem still around in the Church today.
>
> I've learned that Paul wanted to bring the cross of Christ into the heart of the Corinthian church's life.

However, he saw the cross not simply as something that happened to Jesus but also the pattern for how God continues to work in his world.

I've learned that Paul's stories of his own hardship are not indulgent accounts to make his readers feel sorry for him. Rather, they are modelling how God continues to choose the pattern of the cross to work in our lives today.

I've learned that for Paul, God is at work in so many more places than we think. He is at work in the cross-shaped places and not just the places where everything is going well.

I've learned that when we go against the cultural flow and open up about our tough stuff, we are actually telling the story of the cross in our generation, and offering encouragement and hope.

I've found that exploring these passages has helped me make more sense of how God was at work in some of the tough places I have seen and experienced. They have not given me easy answers to difficult and painful questions, but they have persuaded me that God can be active in the most unpromising places. And that has given me an invitation to be more real in my communication with others, at home, at work and in the church. (Plyming, *Being Real*, 6–7)

We all want to be rewarded with good things for doing what is good. It's American, it's human. We even have biblical support (Deuteronomy 28). But then there's Jesus who suffered. We need the realism of George Orwell, about whom and about which his biographer, Gordon Bowker, wrote: Orwell "saw a contradiction at the heart of the [Christendom] system [in which he grew up]—'Broadly, you were taught to be a good Christian and a social success, which is impossible'" (Bowker, *Inside George Orwell*, 32).

Paul did not believe God exploited humans to cause sufferings and hardships. Paul was not blaming God. Rather, Paul learned about God and about the way of the cross *in and through* his hardships. He coped through his suffering by pondering and participating in the cross.

CHRIST'S FOOL

To begin today's reading, Paul returns to his ironic usage of "fool" and "boast." He turns both completely upside down. The Corinthians convinced themselves that they were "wise," and that the movement of Paul was "foolish," so Paul flipped the script by embracing foolishness and turning wisdom into the wisdom of the cross of Christ (1 Corinthians 1:17, 18–30; 2:1, 4–7, 13; 3:19; 2 Corinthians 1:12). Guy Nave gets it right when he writes that Paul, "feeling as though he has no choice but to stoop to the level of his opponents," began to boast (Nave, *2 Corinthians*, 326). That flipped script turned his boasting from what he had accomplished, from a Roman point of view, into boasting about his sufferings and weaknesses. His "Let no one take me for a fool" shows he knows he's not a fool. Yet, he flips it by saying "then tolerate me just as you would a fool" since he knows they think he's a fool (11:16). Perhaps a way of saying this is that Paul *redefined* the word "foolishness" when he framed the cross as God's kind of foolishness, and that kind of foolishness Paul heartily embraced. If not playfully at times.

BOASTING FOR "CHRIST'S FOOL"

So, Paul ventures into a list of items to "boast" about as Christ's fool. What he has to say is not what "the Lord would" say but only what Christ's fool has to say. Since *Romanitas* expects boasting in one's status and accomplishments, he will too—but he will boast about what they consider reckless foolishness. He gets snarky, so it seems, violating his promise at 10:1 when he says "To my shame I admit that we were too weak" to absorb their abuse of him (11:21). His boasting then goes on for a dozen or so verses, with one interruption at 11:30–31.

He boasts about his Hebrew, Israelite, and Abrahamic *heritage* (11:22). He boasts about his *gospel calling and mission*. In fact, he claims "more" when it comes to ministry: "I have worked much harder, been in prison more frequently, been flogged more severely, and been exposed to death again and again" (11:23).

His *persecutions and physical beatings* must have made for a body marked by scars and perhaps broken bones now changing the shape of his arms and legs. Notice these: "Five times I received from the Jews the forty lashes minus one. Three times I was beaten with rods, once I was pelted with stones" (11:24–25). You and I may acquire some anxiety over an airplane going down or over a car accident but notice *the perils of travel* for Paul in which he boasts: "Three times I was shipwrecked, I spent a night and a day in the open sea, I have been constantly on the move. I have been in danger from rivers, in danger from bandits, in danger from my fellow Jews, in danger from Gentiles; in danger in the city, in danger in the country, in danger at sea; and in danger from false believers" (11:25–26). I am editing this paragraph on the island of Naxos, Greece. Kris and I spend our time looking at the waves, sometimes tumultuous, that shaped Paul's own hardships.

And add now his escape from Antioch (11:32–33). Have you ever wondered about the size of the apostle Paul when you read he was let down from the wall in a basket? Why, you may have asked, did Paul say his fellow Jews persecuted him? Because his gospel drew gentiles out of their civil religion and socially respectable way of life, which got Jewish folks into trouble with the authorities, and he led some Jewish believers in Jesus into tension with those who did not turn to Jesus as Messiah. What Paul does not mention here but is everywhere hidden in plain sight is that *the people of wherever Paul planted a church thought Paul was a social pest.* They were right, as he would say, and then he'd turn "pest" into a new Christian term!

We are not surprised he then boasts about his *physical exhaustions*: he was sleep- and food-deprived (11:27). Surely leaders of all sorts, not excluding ministry leaders, resonate with his boasting again about *the pressures of serving and supervising people:* "There is my daily supervision, that is, the anxiety for all the assemblies" (11:28; *Second Testament*). All these pressures and exhaustions are complicated by another source of boasting: his *empathies*. He feels weak when others are weak, and he is lit up when faith collapses in those he loves (11:29).

So, his principle for boasting finally comes to the surface: "If I must boast, I will boast of the things that show my weakness" (11:30). He pulls God into the letter: God "knows I am not lying" about both all he has experienced and that he has chosen to flip the Corinthian script to boast in the weaknesses (11:31). Paul learned through all his experiences that the way to perceive his hardships was not to form a culture of complaint. No, he learned to draw upon the embodied life of Jesus as he strove for justice in each situation. And often failed to get the latter as he succeeded in the former. Paul does not glorify suffering; he glorifies the God who carried him through the hardships. What he does not boast about was a virtue he could have put at the top of his list: courage. Which is why he exhorted the Corinthians not to lose heart (4:1, 16).

It's hard to know how the Corinthians responded. If one thinks chapters ten through thirteen echo or actually are the Severe Letter, then we can be assured they were won over by Paul. If not, we can infer that their former positive response to Titus was repeated after reading this portion of 2 Corinthians. We could also guess they turned away from Paul. That this letter survived suggests they were won over. Suffering by believers becomes a witness to the oppressor that can do deep work, and no one pierced into the heart of this view of suffering more than Dietrich Bonhoeffer, who wrote in his famous book on *Discipleship*, that "by suffering, the disciple will bring evil to its end and thus will overcome the evil person. Suffering willingly endured is stronger than evil; it is the death of evil" (Bonhoeffer, *Discipleship*, 134).

IMITATING PAUL

Theoretically, we can enjoy the ironic rhetoric of Paul's. We can back off and mutter, *He sure gave 'em a good one there!* But that little experience of "he got 'em good" gets us off the hook too easily. So, let me imitate Paul with a make-believe mom called Phoebe. Phoebe, out of her commitment to Jesus and the way of the cross, commits herself to a life of serving others, to justice, and to peace.

Phoebe married Ben while they were in graduate school, and they set up a home in the suburbs. Phoebe and Ben chose to move to the inner city of Chicago to dwell among those who were poor and disadvantaged. Phoebe and Ben had two children, one girl and one boy. Phoebe chose to place her children in the public schools, and because of a lack of funding in the schools, she and Ben did some extra schooling most evenings. Over time, Phoebe engaged in serving at a homeless shelter, in attending aldermen meetings in the neighborhood. She became known in the community for her grace, for her peace efforts, for mentoring young mothers, and for her wildly popular Sunday school class.

So popular was she that she was invited to a wealthy suburb's megachurch to speak about caring for the poor. She boasted about her 1,000 square foot apartment. She boasted about growing her own food because they lived in a food desert. She boasted about the danger of walking the streets late at night. She boasted about her lack of stylish clothing and eating only bread and soup three nights a week so they could give more to the community. She boasted about taking those who had overdosed to the hospital, spending the night in the emergency room, and about helping the addict back to her apartment. She boasted about knowing the sounds of gun shots and that they had a window shot out one night. And she boasted about growing up rich and growing up born again, and both had become idols that needed to be broken. Phoebe was not white. She was not invited back to speak again. But two families from that suburban church soon moved into her neighborhood.

QUESTIONS FOR REFLECTION AND APPLICATION

1. How does the pattern of the cross still serve as the pattern for how God works in the world today?

2. What did pondering the cross teach Paul about his own sufferings?

3. How does Paul redefine "foolishness" in light of the cross?

4. Could you reorient some of your own suffering into boasting in such a way that it glorifies the God who carried you through the hardships?

5. What people groups awaken your compassion? Whose weaknesses cause you to feel weak?

FOR FURTHER READING

Dietrich Bonhoeffer, *Discipleship*, Dietrich Bonhoeffer Works 4 (Minneapolis: Fortress, 2001).

Gordon Bowker, *Inside George Orwell* (New York: Palgrave Macmillan, 2003).

THE THORN IN OUR FLESH ABOUT PAUL'S

2 Corinthians 12:1–10

[1] *I must go on boasting. Although there is nothing to be gained, I will go on to visions and revelations from the Lord.* [2] *I know a man in Christ who fourteen years ago was caught up to the third heaven. Whether it was in the body or out of the body I do not know—God knows.* [3] *And I know that this man—whether in the body or apart from the body I do not know, but God knows—*[4] *was caught up to paradise and heard inexpressible things, things that no one is permitted to tell.* [5] *I will boast about a man like that, but I will not boast about myself, except about my weaknesses.* [6] *Even if I should choose to boast, I would not be a fool, because I would be speaking the truth. But I refrain, so no one will think more of me than is warranted by what I do or say,* [7] *or because of these surpassingly great revelations. Therefore, in order to keep me from becoming conceited, I was given a thorn in my flesh, a messenger of Satan, to torment me.* [8] *Three times I pleaded with the Lord to take it away from me.* [9] *But he said to me, "My grace is sufficient for you, for my power is made perfect in weakness." Therefore I will boast all the more gladly about my weaknesses, so that Christ's power may rest on me.* [10] *That is why, for Christ's sake, I delight in weaknesses, in insults, in hardships, in persecutions, in difficulties. For when I am weak, then I am strong.*

Those who have ecstatic religious experiences, which are often life-changing experiences, both know their potency in one's life but also their ability to alienate a person from others. Since others have not had such an experience, those others can wonder what they lack, while those who have such intense religious moments can become conceited about their religious experiences. Some have intense moments more than once, some often, and some seem to be able to put themselves into a position of having such experiences when they want them. Such persons are at times called "mystics." Even to talk about such ecstasies can become uncomfortable for those with the experience. Paul's ironic boasting in chapter eleven takes a turn around a corner and up to the mountain top to describe his third person account of ecstasy, that is, of being "caught up to the third heaven" to see "visions and revelations" (12:1–3). That he did not have such experiences often could be indicated by his need to appeal an experience some fourteen years earlier (12:2).

BOASTING

It's likely Paul's complainers had sufficient spiritual experiences to boast about them. Perhaps they used them to compare themselves with Paul. Perhaps they persuaded some Corinthians of their superiority because of their experiences. Mystical experiences have a way of convincing others of the mystic's importance. So, Paul appeals to his experience, this time boasting in such a way that eliminates the braggadocio. One hard-to-avoid way to read today's passage looks like this: *Paul could brag on and on about his heavenly journey and his various experiences* (see Sidebar), *but he has to spend all his time fighting off his weaknesses, his "thorn in the flesh," and dealing with complainers and people out to get him.*

Paul's discomfort about talking about his experience makes him talk about himself like this: "I know a man . . . whether it was in the body or out of the body I do not know . . . And I know this man . . . I will boast about a man like that," which is then chased away with "but I will not boast about myself" (12:2–5). He admits that he could go on about being "caught up to paradise" where he heard "inexpressible things that no one is permitted to tell" (12:4) but chooses instead only to boast about his "weaknesses" and even then, he says, "I refrain" (12:6).

Paul's Revelations, Visions, Ecstasies

I went in response to a *revelation* and, meeting privately with those esteemed as leaders, I presented to them the gospel that I preach among the Gentiles. I wanted to be sure I was not running and had not been running my race in vain (Galatians 2:2).

As he neared Damascus on his journey, suddenly a light from heaven flashed around him. He fell to the ground and heard a voice say to him, "Saul, Saul, why do you persecute me?"

"Who are you, Lord?" Saul asked.

"I am Jesus, whom you are persecuting," he replied. "Now get up and go into the city, and you will be told what you must do."

The men traveling with Saul stood there speechless; they heard the sound but did not see anyone. Saul got up from the ground, but when he opened his eyes he could see nothing. So they led him by the hand into Damascus. For three days he was blind, and did not eat or drink anything (Acts 9:3–9).

Then Barnabas went to Tarsus to look for Saul, and when he found him, he brought him to Antioch. So for a whole year Barnabas and Saul met with the church and taught great numbers of people. The disciples were called Christians first at Antioch (Acts 11:25–26).

During the night Paul had a vision of a man of Macedonia standing and begging him, "Come over to Macedonia and help us." After Paul had seen the vision, we got ready at once to leave for Macedonia, concluding that God had called us to preach the gospel to them (Acts 16:9–10).

One night the Lord spoke to Paul in a vision: "Do not be afraid; keep on speaking, do not be silent. For I am with you, and no one is going to attack and harm you, because I have many people in this city" (Acts 18:9–10).

"When I returned to Jerusalem and was praying at the temple, I fell into a trance and saw the Lord speaking to me. 'Quick!' he said. 'Leave Jerusalem immediately, because the people here will not accept your testimony about me.'

"'Lord,' I replied, 'these people know that I went from one synagogue to another to imprison and beat those who believe in you. And when the blood of your martyr Stephen was shed, I stood there giving my approval and guarding the clothes of those who were killing him.'

"Then the Lord said to me, 'Go; I will send you far away to the Gentiles.'" (Acts 22:17–21).

Based on Murray Harris, *2 Corinthians*, 836–837.

You may wonder if his "I know a man" is a way of talking about himself. He ends the wondering when he gives it away in verse seven where he is speaking of himself and his "surpassingly great revelations." If you compare the third person of 12:2 with the first person of 12:3–4, you see that Paul has pulled off the third person mask. The language is nearly identical. When in 12:5, Paul says "I will not boast about myself," he has again unmasked the third person account of ecstasy. He does not boast about his extraordinary experiences because he's spoken of them indirectly, only in the third person. Despite a small leak of the identity of the "I know a man," he was full-on with the first person ("I") when he spoke of his hardships (11:21–33). Today's passage only works if the ecstasy is Paul's experience that is cut down by God with the thorn about which Paul talks in 12:7–10. One only needs a thorn if one has something that needs to be tempered.

Still, Paul knows he can boast about his heritage (11:22–23; Philippians 3:4–6) and his ecstasy (2 Corinthians 12:1–6), but God has done something to him that prevents him from glorifying himself. The deepest Christian truth for Paul is to know the power of God, the power of the cross of Christ at work in him in the midst of hardships and suffering. In that work, he draws closest to Christ. Instead of touting his accomplishments, and there were many, instead of acting like the Corinthians who were acting like the Romans, Paul chose to glory in the cross of Christ. What was foolish to his critics was precious to him. He saw in his weaknesses, including what he had learned so far with the thorn in the flesh, the secret to his spiritual growth and formation.

WITH A THORN

Big temptations for the leader are pride and status. Paul knew his abundant successes carried the power to carry him up the social stairs to honor and glory. To a big platform. To fame and celebrity. But God had to teach Paul something about social climbing. Paul understands what he calls a "thorn-piercing-the-flesh" (McKnight, *Second Testament*) as a gift from God that was exploited by Satan to prevent him from social climbing. Our thorn in the flesh is figuring out Paul's thorn in the flesh. The term leads us to a thorn or a splinter. Either works.

I rely on my seminary professor, Murray Harris, for what we can definitely know about Paul's thorn: (1) it came after his ecstatic revelations; (2) it caused pain; (3) God gave it, Satan exploited it; (4) it was permanent; (5) it was humbling; (6) it led to social degradation; and (7) it made Paul feel helpless or weak (Harris, *2 Corinthians*, 857). So, what was it? Again, from Harris: perhaps some kind of anxiety, perhaps opposition to Paul wherever he went, or perhaps some physical symptom (like malaria, bad vision, or migraine headaches) (Harris, 858–859). For Harris the best guess, and guess it is, is some kind of physical symptom that kept him in check. Here's what matters most, as put into bold words by Barbara Brown Taylor: "this spiritual giant had something physical going on with him that bugged him every day of his life" (Taylor, *Home by Another Way*, 173). Yes, it bugged him. Nothing like something bugging you all day long. Like a bad back, or arthritis in your fingers, or a tendency toward vertigo. Especially when you know it will never go away.

What matters is that this man of faith took it before God with pleadings and requests. His experience of the ongoing thorn taught him that God was saying *Deal with it*. Which simply drove Paul right back to the cross of Christ and the lesson of power through weakness. Verse ten just might be the window one needs to catch a glimpse of Paul's thorn: "I delight in weaknesses, in insults, in hardships, in persecutions, in difficulties" (12:10). Perhaps, too, the thorn was

151

a constant experience of opposition to his gospel work. Perhaps it was the Corinthians! Judy Diehl is right: "Perhaps it is better that we do not know exactly what it was" (Diehl, *2 Corinthians*, 370).

QUESTIONS FOR REFLECTION AND APPLICATION

1. How does Paul balance his supernatural ecstasies and his physical weaknesses in his writing to the Corinthians?

2. What are your thoughts on what Paul's thorn in the flesh might have been?

3. How did Paul's struggles bring him closer to Jesus?

4. What would it look like for you to "glory in the cross of Christ"?

5. What do your critics find foolish about you? How could this be reclaimed in a positive way?

FOR FURTHER READING

Barbara Brown Taylor, *Home by Another Way* (Lanham: Rowman and Littlefield, 1999).

FEELING BAD AFTER DOING WHAT YOU THOUGHT WAS RIGHT

2 Corinthians 12:11–21

[11] I have made a fool of myself, but you drove me to it. I ought to have been commended by you, for I am not in the least inferior to the "super-apostles," even though I am nothing. [12] I persevered in demonstrating among you the marks of a true apostle, including signs, wonders and miracles. [13] How were you inferior to the other churches, except that I was never a burden to you? Forgive me this wrong!

[14] Now I am ready to visit you for the third time, and I will not be a burden to you, because what I want is not your possessions but you. After all, children should not have to save up for their parents, but parents for their children. [15] So I will very gladly spend for you everything I have and expend myself as well. If I love you more, will you love me less? [16] Be that as it may, I have not been a burden to you. Yet, crafty fellow that I am, I caught you by trickery! [17] Did I exploit you through any of the men I sent to you? [18] I urged Titus to go to you and I sent our brother with him. Titus did not exploit you, did he? Did we not walk in the same footsteps by the same Spirit?

[19] Have you been thinking all along that we have been defending

ourselves to you? We have been speaking in the sight of God as those in Christ; and everything we do, dear friends, is for your strengthening. [20] *For I am afraid that when I come I may not find you as I want you to be, and you may not find me as you want me to be. I fear that there may be discord, jealousy, fits of rage, selfish ambition, slander, gossip, arrogance and disorder.* [21] *I am afraid that when I come again my God will humble me before you, and I will be grieved over many who have sinned earlier and have not repented of the impurity, sexual sin and debauchery in which they have indulged.*

The tension between Paul and the Corinthians, or at least some of them, has not been relieved. Writing the last two and a half chapters has not resolved it for Paul. He still wonders how they will respond. His inability to put the unresolved issues to rest indicates the depth of his relational trauma. In today's passage, he begins to question himself.

I believe we see a Paul who feels bad after doing what he thought was right. He has pleaded with them. He sent Titus and one other and perhaps he sent another letter with them (12:18).* He has defended himself point-by-point. One has to wonder if Paul was wondering if this portion of the letter has gone too far. He clearly waffles on what he is doing: he's a "fool" for how he's defending himself. He blames the Corinthians: "you drove me to it" (12:11). So, he returns one more time to the complainers and their complaints. As you read, you may sense he is wandering into complaints and then moving out of them with defenses that reveal more complaints he needs to defend. You may also sense an unrelenting, intense quarrel.

---

* Depending on what one concludes about 10–13: if it is the Severe Letter, the third companion did not go with Titus to Corinth. If chapters 10–13 are originally a fresh draft after even more news from Corinth, Paul sent Titus ahead with one brother to Corinth.

THE COMPLAINTS

No new complaints appear in today's passage. The complainers think:

1. Paul is inferior to their superior super-apostles;
2. they resent that he refused to receive support from the Corinthians;
3. they don't believe he loves them as he loves other churches;
4. they think he is "crafty" and uses "trickery";
5. and they believe he exploited them by sending Titus and the other brother (12:11–17).

We've read about each of these already. It appears the Corinthians didn't like anything he did. Or that they found something wrong about every decision he made. Or just call it sealioning, which Wikipedia defines as follows:

> Sealioning (also sea-lioning and sea lioning) is a type of trolling or harassment that consists of pursuing people with relentless requests for evidence, often tangential or previously addressed, while maintaining a pretense of civility and sincerity ("I'm just trying to have a debate"), and feigning ignorance of the subject matter (URL at the end of this chapter).

Or perhaps there was something to some of their complaints. Or perhaps there was a divisive party spirit at work in Corinth and Paul was trying to figure out how to respond "Yes" and "Perhaps" to each of these perhaps. Leaders in churches at times experience exhaustion in responding to the complaints because they realize the complainers themselves are the problem. Not always, but sometimes. Leaders at times realize that regardless of the response, a new complaint pops up in its place. One can only engage "deny, deny, deny" so long. At times, also, leaders realize they are hearing complaints but have not gotten to the bottom of it. They begin to ask over and over, *What's really going on here?*

You may wonder, as many of us do, what has become of the warm feelings that shaped the first seven chapters. Those chapters expressed such vulnerability and mutual affection. If the Severe Letter had done its work, why now so much more of the same in 10–13? Understanding these chapters as an echo or even the Severe Letter best explains the ending chapters of this letter. Or perhaps a traumatized Paul just can't get over how he has been treated. A sign of trauma is the need to return to the pain and talk about it over and over. Only by returning to the pain, only by facing it over and over, does one understand it and get through it, around it, or beyond it. Paul was working it out in these last chapters of this letter.

SELF-DEFENSE, SORT OF

We learn even more about Paul and the Corinthians when we give careful attention to Paul's defense of himself. Second thoughts about what he has just written haunt him. We observe somewhat of an internally tortured apostle here. He has chosen a strategy and is not so sure it's working, but he continues anyway.

He says, "I have made a fool of myself." Even if he defines *fool* as walking in the way of the cross in a world shaped by status, he admits that they "drove" him to defending himself. They should be affirming his gifts and status with them. So once again, he claims he is not one bit inferior to these supposed "super-apostles" they think are so gifted. He turns to the cross because he doesn't want to play their game when he writes "even though I am nothing" (12:11). In his own defense he can say he has proven his calling because they saw the "marks of a true apostle," which after all included "signs, wonders and miracles" (12:12). They ought to count in his favor. The other marks were both seeing Jesus Christ personally and being commissioned by Jesus Christ. One objective look at the evidence, in other words, confirms the calling of Paul to the Corinthians. Yet, as he reflects on his innermost self, Paul wants to make a distinction out of something different: his self-defense is not for himself but for God, and for them. They see a distinction without a difference. Self-defense, they say, is self-defense. Self-defense, Paul says back to them, is not always self-defense!

Again, they think he has shown more love to other churches than to theirs (12:13). Love in this case means receiving financial support from the Corinthians. That theme, support, requires Paul to offer a longer response. His explanation is that he chose not to be a "burden" on them (12:13, 14, 16) and "burden" echoes in "exploit" (12:17, 18). Paul did not receive support from churches he planted until they were mature enough spiritually and financially to be self-sufficient. So, he had no hesitations receiving support from Ephesus or Philippi or Macedonia (Thessaloniki), but when it came to Corinth he chose not to. Their divisions, their complaints, their leaders needed growth. Their pride in being able to announce in this wannabe Rome kind of city blocked for Paul any willingness to take their offerings. They were shamed by his refusal, and he was adamant in his stance.

His wandering in and out of their complaints continues. His explanation of not wanting to burden them was not received well. So, he defends it in today's passage. He did not want their money; he wanted them. Just like parents and children (12:14). Just like wives and husbands, too. He turns to a personal, emotional appeal: he was more than happy to "spend for you everything I have and expend myself as well." He continues with sharper words: "If I love you more, will you love me less?" (12:15). His more-love was not being a burden, but they saw it as less-love. Perhaps the crafty and trickery terms are connected to this economic decision by Paul. He denies both complaints and then denies their complaint about exploiting them through the messengers (12:17–18).

Second thoughts or not, Paul wonders aloud if the Corinthians think "we have been defending ourselves to you?" (12:19). Of course they do. Yet, Paul wants to make clear that "we have been speaking in the sight of God as those in Christ." That is, his self-defense is not shaped to acquire status and honor for his work. He wants all the credit to go to God. Furthermore, all he does is "for your strengthening" (12:19).

HIS VISIT

Paul's visits to Corinth, along with visits by his own messengers, are packed with pastoral anxiety. He knows himself well enough to reveal his anxiety when he says "I am afraid" twice (12:20, 21). He's afraid they won't like him any longer. He says it in a tidy little poetic set of two lines:

> I may not find you as I want you to be,
>   and you may not find me as you want me
> to be.

He's also afraid he may discover the divisions he discussed in 1 Corinthians 1–4 will arise again with "discord, jealousy, fits of rage, selfish ambition, slander, gossip, arrogance and disorder" (2 Corinthians 12:20). The NIV's terms don't quite reveal the competitiveness and status-mongering at work. For "selfish ambition" I have "status seekings," for "arrogance" I have "using natural status" (McKnight, *Second Testament*). He fears the problems of claiming status over others in 1 Corinthians are unresolved (see *1 Corinthians*, Introduction, pp. 1–16).

He is also afraid he will be humbled and grieved over the condition of the house churches in Corinth (12:21). In addition to the sinful behaviors Paul criticized in his previous letter, he's afraid he will be grieved "over many who have sinned earlier and have not repented." He names the sins that take us back to 1 Corinthians 5 and probably 1 Corinthians 6, too: "impurity, sexual sin and debauchery [flaunting sexuality] in which they have indulged" (2 Corinthians 12:21; words in bracket are from *Second Testament*). Is anxiety speaking here? Is a bit of paranoia speaking here? Or does he know more than he lets on? Experience has informed Paul about human behaviors, and I suspect it's more about what he knows than his imagined fear.

WHAT TO DO?

I finish reading these three chapters with a heavy heart for Paul, for the Corinthians, for pastoral care leaders today, and for churches. (And we are not done. There's more in chapter thirteen.) I feel for Paul. He has written from his heart but is not entirely sure that what he has done was the right thing to do. Nor is he confident the Corinthians will respond as he thinks they ought. No wonder in his list of hardships he includes "daily the pressure of my concern for all the churches" (11:28). Paul was empathic, and empathic persons deeply care how others feel. The Corinthians' feelings for Paul pierced his heart with pain.

The ways of the Corinthians are as American as they were Roman. The Corinthians had a culture problem, one that could be called a complaint culture and a status culture. Paul saw their problem as a cross problem. How to get out of that cultural mess? In a book I have recently written with my daughter called *Pivot*, we sketch a process for churches to pivot from toxic cultures into *tov* (goodness) cultures. We name three priorities: focus on character formation, use power the way Jesus wants, and be a personal example. Then three pivotal practices: build a coalition of those committed to tov, take one step at a time, and create pockets of tov. Then three powers: keep in mind the power of a congregation's culture to create people who fit in that culture, rely on the power of the Spirit, and anchor the changes in the grace of God (McKnight, Barringer, *Pivot*). Transformation is a long-term commitment, full of hard and difficult work. What you will discover is that Paul is with you! He may well be listening in to see if he got it right.

QUESTIONS FOR REFLECTION AND APPLICATION

1. What new complaints about Paul now come up?

2. Do you think his critics had valid complaints or were they just determined to think the worst of Paul?

3. Why doesn't Paul accept financial support from the Corinthians?

4. When have you felt bad about doing something you thought was right? How did the situation resolve?

5. In what areas of your Christian life have you felt "daily pressure of concern"? What could you do to turn that over to God today?

FOR FURTHER READING

Scot McKnight, Laura Barringer, *Pivot: The Priorities, Practices, and Powers That Can Transform Your Church into a Tov Culture* (Carol Stream: Tyndale Elevate, 2023).
Sealioning: https://en.wikipedia.org/wiki/Sealioning

I'LL ARRIVE SOON

2 Corinthians 13:1–14

¹ This will be my third visit to you. "Every matter must be established by the testimony of two or three witnesses." ² I already gave you a warning when I was with you the second time. I now repeat it while absent: On my return I will not spare those who sinned earlier or any of the others, ³ since you are demanding proof that Christ is speaking through me. He is not weak in dealing with you, but is powerful among you. ⁴ For to be sure, he was crucified in weakness, yet he lives by God's power. Likewise, we are weak in him, yet by God's power we will live with him in our dealing with you.

⁵ Examine yourselves to see whether you are in the faith; test yourselves. Do you not realize that Christ Jesus is in you—unless, of course, you fail the test? ⁶ And I trust that you will discover that we have not failed the test. ⁷ Now we pray to God that you will not do anything wrong—not so that people will see that we have stood the test but so that you will do what is right even though we may seem to have failed. ⁸ For we cannot do anything against the truth, but only for the truth. ⁹ We are glad whenever we are weak but you are strong; and our prayer is that you may be fully restored. ¹⁰ This is why I write these things when I am absent, that when I come I may not have to be harsh in my use of authority—the authority the Lord gave me for building you up, not for tearing you down.

[11] *Finally, brothers and sisters, rejoice! Strive for full restoration, encourage one another, be of one mind, live in peace. And the God of love and peace will be with you.*

[12] *Greet one another with a holy kiss. [13] All God's people here send their greetings.*

[14] *May the grace of the Lord Jesus Christ, and the love of God, and the fellowship of the Holy Spirit be with you all.*

To avoid direct confrontations, Paul has sent Titus at least once to Corinth. Titus had the gifts of pastoral care and empathy. His gifts were put to use in order for Paul to arrive with his gifts and pastoral care. So, he announces in this letter that he is himself coming soon, which he calls his "third visit" (Acts 20:2 records it). He could not have written this (our) last chapter without his imagination creating some anxiety and, depending on how the Corinthians respond to this letter, they will have heard this with affection or anxiety. The second visit he made entailed "warning" and the last page or so of this letter includes a repetition of that warning (2 Corinthians 13:2). But he wants, as far as he is able, to warn in a state of weakness, in a state of dependence on God's Spirit, and in a state of walking in the way of the cross. It's hard to threaten a church with discipline in a way that reflects the weakness of the cross. Today's reading is Paul's attempt to do just that.

A word about the success of this letter. If you read Acts 20:2's record of the third visit, you get the impression that a three-month stay in Corinth, after this letter had been sent, suggests the Corinthians responded as they should have. It's an impression, but one worth pondering affirmatively.

The Warning of Paul

Paul cleverly, if not compellingly, connects the necessity of two or three witnesses with his second and third visits to

Corinth (13:1). He warned them on the second visit and will
do so again during his imminent third visit, about the sinners
who have not repented (cf. 1 Corinthians 5–6; 2 Corinthians
12:21). Everything about this opening hinges on tone and
on where the Corinthians are spiritually: Paul wants to
be humble and gentle (10:1), but these words sound like a
threat. If the Corinthians have begun a process of dealing
with the sinners, then they will receive these words of Paul as
deserved rebuke. If they still think he's their problem, then
they will hear the words as the threat of an authoritarian.

He brings this warning theme up again in 13:10 with
words that have shifted more into the mode of hope. When
he arrives, he doesn't want to pull out his authority card, even
though the Lord has given him authority. And to remind
them, that authority was not for "demolition" but for their
"formation" (13:10; *Second Testament*).

THE CONDITION OF PAUL

Paul only wants to be heard as nothing more than an agent
of Christ. He writes "you are demanding proof that Christ
is speaking through me." Even more, he appeals to his weakness and need for dependence on Christ, who is "not weak
in dealing with you, but is powerful among you" (13:3). He
makes an analogy between Christ and himself: as Christ was
crucified in weakness and was powerfully raised from the
dead, so Paul is weak in himself but powerful when Christ
uses him to speak to the Corinthians (13:4).

Guy Nave records a beautiful reminder about what
weakness can do positively, and even negatively, for those
who benefit from another's weakness:

> Virtually all of the young men and women I grew up
> with who made it to college were raised by parents

who did not attend college. Many of our parents never even finished high school. Our parents struggled, suffered, and worked long hours to provide us with opportunities they never had. Many of us are now strong, successful professionals. While most of us realize that our "strength" is a direct result of their "weakness," there are some who, as a result of their strength, are now ashamed of their parents' weakness. (Nave, *2 Corinthians*, 329)

Maybe we need to pause to ponder who carried us by surrendering themselves to weaknesses so we could become strong. Paul is one of those. He chose to be weak so the Corinthians could become strong, but they have despised him for it. They gaslit the man. It hurt.

EXHORTATIONS

Paul's letters always finish off with some exhortations. First, the exhortation to examine yourself takes precedence (13:5–6). Are they "in the faith" or not? This is quite the measure. He fully believes the Corinthian complainers must decide among and about themselves whether they are followers of Jesus or not. If they are, Christ indwells them and will lead them out of this divisiveness, this status-mongering, this intoxication with *Romanitas*, and this casual disregard of blatant sexual immoralities in the church. In the process of self-examination, they will be deciding at the same time if Paul is in the right. Which means Paul draws a line in the sand: *Either you stand with me in my weakness in trusting in Christ or you stand against me and the way of the cross.* Just wow. I know very few pastors, parents, and church leaders who have not had similar conversations. One can't be for Christ and against Christ at the same time. Such conversations require love, empathy, and follow-up. But such conversations will be had and will be hard.

Second, do what is right (13:7). This strikes us as a bit obvious until we realize it's all based on a prayer Paul is formulating. He is praying they will do what is right once they have examined themselves. Once again, his weakness breaks through: he doesn't want them to do what is right to prove his self-examination exhortation was the right thing to do. No, even if they think he's been a flop in how he has treated them, he wants them to do what is right because it's right to do! At work here is that Paul does not want the glory if they do the right thing and choose the way of the cross. He's committed to the truth, nothing else (13:8), and the truth means he's on the weak side and they are on the strong side (13:9). So, his letter was written to exhort them to be "restored" and at peace with the ways of Christ (13:10).

SEALED WITH A KISS (OR A SIDE HUG)

We come to the end of the second of Paul's letters to the Corinthians. At least the second that has survived. The themes have not changed much since the opening of 1 Corinthians, and probably since his arrival more than five years earlier than 2 Corinthians. He wants them to rejoice and even more to be "prepared" for his arrival (13:11; *Second Testament*). The NIV's "Strive for full restoration" suggests too much the theme of reconciliation. The term Paul uses is about being ready. But good relations, sealed with a kiss, are very much at the heart of all he says in 13:11, which he anchors in the "love-and-peace-God" (McKnight, *Second Testament*).

He ends at 13:14 with one of the most beautiful, trinitarian grace-prayers ever written. We call them "benedictions," which means to speak good words over someone. To wish them well. But they are much more significant than our customary wishes, like "God bless" or the less theological "blessings." This benediction falls upon Christians gathered together and unites them into a God who is Three-in-One. And it falls upon us so we can participate in the gospel story— the story about Jesus Christ who is the Lord, the story about a God who is love and who loves us, and the story about the Spirit who is turning us from an "I" into a "We." I reformatted it to show this wonderful benediction's poetic features:

> May
> > the grace of the Lord Jesus Christ,
> > and the love of God,
> > and the fellowship of the Holy Spirit
> > > be with you all.

Each of those prayer requests, if absorbed by the Corinthians or by us, will lead them and us into unity with one another.

QUESTIONS FOR REFLECTION AND APPLICATION

1. How does Paul walk the line between warning them from a position of authority and walking in the weakness of the cross?

2. What does Paul expect of the Corinthians for them to show their allegiance to the way of Jesus?

3. How do you think the Corinthians responded to Paul's pleas?

4. As you finish this study, contemplate whether there is correction you need to give, or one you need to receive?

5. Read Paul's closing benediction out loud and imagine Paul praying it for you. Receive the blessing.

New Testament Everyday Bible Study Series

Become a daily Bible reader attentive to the mind of God

In the New Testament Everyday Bible Study Series, each volume:
- offers brief expositions of the biblical text and offers a clear focus for the central message of each passage;
- brings the passage alive with fresh images and what it means to follow King Jesus;
- provides biblical connections and questions for reflection and application for each passage.

HarperChristian Resources

The Blue Parakeet, 2nd Edition

Rethinking How You Read the Bible

Scot McKnight, author of
The Jesus Creed

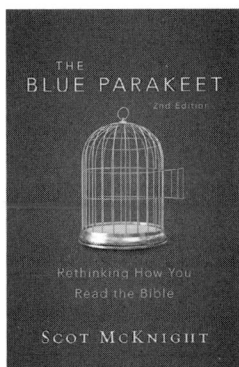

How are we to live out the Bible today? In this updated edition of *The Blue Parakeet*, you'll be challenged to see how Scripture transcends culture and time, and you'll learn how to come to God's Word with a fresh heart and mind.

The gospel is designed to be relevant in every culture, in every age, in every language. It's fully capable of this, and, as we read Scripture, we are called to discern how God is speaking to us today.

And yet applying its words and directions on how to live our lives is not as easy as it seems. As we talk to the Christians around us about issues that matter, many of us wonder: how on earth are we reading the same Bible? How is it that two of us can sit down with the same Bible and come away with two entirely different answers about everything from charismatic gifts to the ordaining of women?

Professor and author of *The King Jesus Gospel* Scot McKnight challenges us to rethink how to read the Bible, not just to puzzle it together into some systematic belief or historical tradition but to see it as an ongoing Story that we're summoned to enter and to carry forward in our day.

What we need is a fresh blowing of God's Spirit on our culture, in our day, and in our ways. We need twenty-first-century Christians living out the biblical gospel in twenty-first-century ways. And if we read the Bible properly, we will see that God never asked one generation to step back in time and live in ways of the past.

Through the Bible, God speaks in each generation, in that generation's ways and beckons us to be a part of his amazing story.

Available in stores and online!

ZONDERVAN

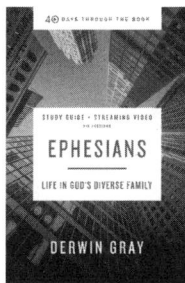

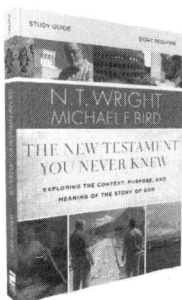

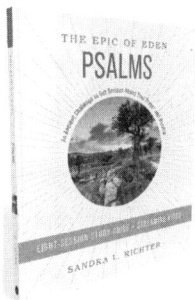

Following King Jesus

We want to follow King Jesus, but do we know how?

Author and professor Scot McKnight will help you discover what it means to follow King Jesus through 24 lessons based on four of his writings (*The King Jesus Gospel*, *The Blue Parakeet – 2nd edition*, *One.Life*, and *A Fellowship of Differents*). McKnight's unique framework for discipleship is designed to be used for personal study and within disciple-making groups of two or more. In this workbook, McKnight will help you:

- Know the biblical meaning of the gospel
- Read the Bible and understand how to apply it today
- Live as disciples of Jesus in all areas of life
- Show the world God's character through life together in the church

Study Guide
9780310105992

Each lesson, created by Becky Castle Miller, has both Personal Study and Group Discussion sections. The Personal Study section contains a discipleship reading from Scot McKnight, an insightful Bible study, and a time for individual prayer, action, and reflection. The Group Discussion section includes discussion questions and activities to do together with a discipleship group. You'll share insights from your personal study time with each other and explore different ways of living out what you're learning.

Whether you have been a Christian for many years or you are desiring a fresh look at what it means to be a disciple, this workbook is an in-depth guide to what it means to follow King Jesus and to discover how to put that kind of life into practice.

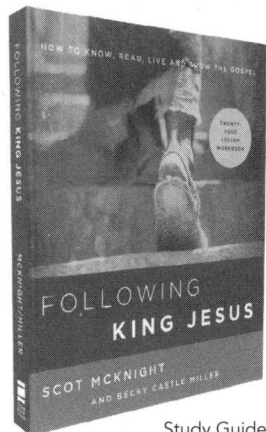

Harper*Christian* Resources